The
Adolescent
Brain

The

Adolescent
Brain

Reaching for Autonomy

Robert Sylwester

CORWIN PRESS
A SAGE Publications Company
Thousand Oaks, CA 91320

Illustrations by Peter Sylwester.

For information:

Corwin Press
A Sage Publications Company
2455 Teller Road
Thousand Oaks, California 91320
www.corwinpress.com

Sage Publications Ltd.
1 Oliver's Yard
55 City Road
London EC1Y 1SP
United Kingdom

Sage Publications India Pvt. Ltd.
B-42, Panchsheel Enclave
Post Box 4109
New Delhi 110 017 India

Printed in the United States of America

Library of Congress Cataloging-in-Publication Data

Sylwester, Robert.
The adolescent brain: Reaching for autonomy/Robert Sylwester.
    p. cm.
Includes bibliographical references and index.
ISBN-13: 978-1-4129-2610-2 (cloth)
ISBN-13: 978-1-4129-2611-9 (pbk.)
    1. Adolescence. 2. Adolescent psychology. 3. Teenagers. I. Title.
HQ796.S967 2007
155.5—dc22

                                            2006029769

This book is printed on acid-free paper.

07   08   09   10   11   10 9 8 7 6 5 4 3 2

Acquisitions Editor:	Faye Zucker
Editorial Assistant:	Gem Rabanera
Production Editor:	Melanie Birdsall
Typesetter:	C&M Digitals (P) Ltd.
Copy Editor:	Bill Bowers
Proofreader:	Cheryl Rivard
Indexer:	John Hulse
Cover Designer:	Michael Dubowe
Graphic Designer:	Lisa Miller

Contents

Preface

Adults who are concerned about the current behavior and future life of an increasingly noncompliant adolescent might wish for a simple, effective resolution of their dilemma, but such an outcome would miss the point of human adolescence.

We get a dozen years at most to make the best case for our values. At about that point, halfway between infant dependency and adult autonomy, our adolescents begin to realize that their adult lives will be spent with nonkin whose values may differ from those of their parents, teachers, and other adults in their lives. Whether we like it or not, our adolescents will then begin to transfer their allegiance to the peers who will accompany them on their journey of self-discovery (as we did a generation earlier). And like it or not, they and their peers will feel more or less untrammeled by our values and wishes (as how we felt a generation earlier). That inevitable adolescent odyssey is the focus of this book.

This book is thus not a *how to do it* book for getting adolescents to continue their reasonably compliant childhood. That's not the point of adolescence. Rather, this book traces the marvelous (and periodically terrifying) extended reach for adult autonomy that characterizes adolescent maturation. We both value and fear those things we can't control—and so we love our adolescents and at the same time fear our loss of control. To understand what's occurring within adolescents doesn't mean that we can control them, any more than understanding meteorology means that we can control a tornado. Still, understanding a phenomenon is much better than not understanding it, and scientists are now providing us with a much clearer understanding of the nature and neurobiology of adolescence.

This knowledge suggests a shift from controlling to mentoring the adolescents in our lives. As a father of seven, a grandfather of 20, and a teacher of many thousands of young folks who were making this odyssey, I've come to realize that seeking to understand adolescence is far more rewarding over the long haul than seeking to control it. That doesn't mean that no useful adolescent mentoring principles exist. This book will suggest general guidelines, but general guidelines aren't *sure-fire* solutions. Parenting and teaching adolescents is currently more an art than a predictable science.

A variety of collaborative adult mentors accompany the adolescent reach for autonomy. Parents, stepparents, and other relatives form one group, and surrogate parents form the other group. Teachers, coaches, and youth program directors are examples of surrogate parents who work principally with groups of adolescents. Counselors, physicians, psychologists, and social workers are examples of surrogate parents who work principally with individual adolescents.

This creates a problem for readers who expect this book to provide specific suggestions related to their particular roles in adolescent mentoring. Advice and activities that one group (such as high school teachers) can effectively use aren't necessarily useful for other groups (such as grandparents or an adolescent's boss). For example, family mentors are very concerned about the long-range implications of behavior, and a police officer may simply want to defuse an angry adolescent confrontation.

This book will thus focus principally on the biological and cultural universals that all mentoring adults must confront. Comparing a cook and a chef might help to clarify things. Both can create nutritious and delicious food. The difference emerges when things go wrong. For example, a recipe-driven cook who lacks an important ingredient can't proceed without it, but a chef who understands the chemistry of ingredients and cooking processes can imaginatively substitute something else for the missing ingredient. A cook is thus dependent on the chef who created the recipe. A chef checks out the available ingredients and the dining situation—and then responds with an appropriate meal.

A book focused on practical mentoring suggestions is thus as limiting as a recipe book (and truth be told, most cooks use only a few of the many useful recipes in a cookbook and ignore the others). A book that seeks rather to explain adolescent development and the culture in which adolescents mature provides the much more useful basic knowledge that a variety of adults can use to mentor adolescents in the specific challenges they confront. This book will contain selected illustrative suggestions, but readers should think of them as seasoning, and not the essence.

That adolescents are influenced by their equally immature peers often creates problems. Although such influence seems a recipe for disaster—and it may periodically be just that—the creative, collaborative explorations of adolescents have also led to many recent advances in computers and in other technologies. Further, each adolescent generation creates its own cultural elements, such as clothing styles and music.

We often think of it as rebellion, but they consider it creativity. Imaginative but rebellious young people have sparked many major scientific advances that contradicted current beliefs. For example, Albert Einstein and Charles Darwin were in their mid-twenties when they did their initial transformational work in physics and biology. James Watson and Francis Crick were graduate students when they discovered DNA. And during high school reunions, we all recall great stories about our own creative adolescent explorations and rebellions. Although we fuss about adolescents, human society has progressed much because of the recurring adolescent belief that there must be a better way of doing things than what adults are currently doing.

The 2006 Winter Olympics are coming to an end as I write this Preface. The virtuoso movements of young people during the past two weeks have fascinated the world. All the athletes had helpful adult coaches, but the coaches could only stand on the sidelines and observe the stumbles and falls that occurred. The athletes had to perform on their own. That's the arrangement for adolescents. We adults can provide mentoring advice, but we can't experience adolescence for another person. We did it on our own, and they will do it on their own—like it or not.

This book thus provides a nontechnical explanation of the underlying neurobiology of adolescence, and then explores the following key developmental phenomena: sexuality and bonding, productivity and vocation, morality and ethics, risks and security, technology and drugs, the arts and humanities, collaboration and autonomy.

I've been teaching and writing for more than a half century, and so I've explored these themes in many different professional settings. This book draws on that experience. I'll tell you about my life and experiences, and that should encourage you to tell your adolescents about your life and experiences, which should encourage them to tell you about their lives and experiences. Getting the cross-generational conversation going is central to mentoring, and to this book. When we adults tell our stories, adolescents will roll their eyes and argue that our experiences are irrelevant to the *more complex* challenges they're confronting—and that's exactly the point of such exchanges. So argue mentally with me as you read about my perhaps *hopelessly dated* experiences and the explanatory models and metaphors I'll use. It will get your creative juices flowing and so help you to connect emerging knowledge about adolescence, universal recurring cultural experiences, and the specific current challenges that you and your adolescents can collaboratively explore.

We're each the world's leading authority on our own experiences and beliefs—and we don't know much more. What adults bring to a discussion is the necessary distance between a related challenge they confronted during their adolescence and their adult perspective of its resolution. What adolescents bring is only the challenge they're currently confronting. Seems like the beginning of a good discussion—if truth and trust are also part of the equation.

It's been interesting this past year to revisit and update what I had earlier thought and written on the issues that constitute this book. I realize that I've matured in my understanding over the years, and it's important for me to recognize the importance of that personal development if I'm going to write about adolescent maturation.

My principal mentors in my own personal odyssey have sequentially been my parents, my siblings, my wife Ruth, and our children. I've further had the opportunity to work with many wonderful colleagues and editors, who helped me to find my professional voice when I was as clueless about a lot of things as the typical adolescent. Many thanks to all of you.

PUBLISHER'S ACKNOWLEDGMENTS

Corwin Press thanks the following reviewers for their contributions to this book:

Renate Caine, Educational Consultant, Caine Learning, Idyllwild, CA

Lisa Edwards, Science Teacher, Hickory High School, Conover, NC

Sheryl Feinstein, Educational Consultant, Augustana College, Sioux Falls, SD

Bob Patterson, Training Manager, Discovery Education, Gig Harbor, WA

Rhonda Spidell, Earth Systems Science Teacher, Albuquerque Academy, Albuquerque, NM

Charre Todd, Teacher, Norman Junior High, Crossett, AR

Patricia Wolfe, Mind Matters, Inc., Educational Consultant, Napa, CA

George Zimmer, Superintendent Richmond School District, Sussex, WI

About the Author

 **Robert Sylwester** is an Emeritus Professor of Education at the University of Oregon who focuses on the educational implications of new developments in science and technology. He is the author of several books and many journal articles. His most recent books are *How to Explain a Brain: An Educator's Handbook of Brain Terms and Cognitive Processes* (Corwin Press, 2005) and *A Biological Brain in a Cultural Classroom: Enhancing Cognitive and Social Development Through Collaborative Classroom Management,* Second Edition (Corwin Press, 2003). Sylwester has received two Distinguished Achievement Awards from The Education Press Association of America for his syntheses of cognitive science research, published in *Educational Leadership.* He has made more than 1,400 conference and inservice presentations on educationally significant developments in brain-stress theory and research. He writes a monthly column for the Internet journal *Brain Connection* (www.brainconnection.com). He can be contacted at bobsyl@uoregon.edu.

ABOUT THE ILLUSTRATOR

Peter Sylwester is a computer graphics designer who developed and adapted the illustrations for this book. His Web site is www.ptrdo.com, and his e-mail address is ptr@ptrdo.com.

CHAPTER ONE

Adolescence in Contemporary Society

Being Somewhat Confused

W e all meander out of childhood into adult life through an adolescent door. Some adolescents go through it relatively easily, but most stumble going over the threshold—their erratic (and alas, often erotic) stumbling being almost a rite of passage.

What's odd is that we adults so often seem surprised and even mystified when we observe adolescents confronting the same problems and doing the same foolish and destructive things we did during our own passage. We often romanticize our own adolescence because we survived it but now worry (as our parents and teachers worried about us) that our children and students won't survive their adolescence—a frequently bewildering puberty-to-maturity period that can simultaneously combine the worst and the best elements of both childhood and adulthood.

Good news: Most adolescents finally make it through the door into responsible adulthood. More good news: We now better understand the underlying biology that drives adolescent maturation.

The several-decades-long ascent of the cognitive neuro-sciences escalated dramatically at about the turn of the 21st century. Important scientific developments have occurred in our understanding of such central concepts as our brain's organization and extended maturation; the biology of emotion, attention, learning, memory, thought, and behavior; and brain plasticity (the physical changes that occur within our brains as we master new challenges).

Furthermore, successful new interventions for children with inadequately developing emotion, attention, and language systems emerged; and potential advances in the stem cell treatment of a wide variety of body/brain maladies sparked both political controversy and parental hope. If such scientific advances can ameliorate many of the school-related maladies that children confront, will that enhance their otherwise more difficult adolescent journey through family and school mazes? Finally, of special interest to educators and parents is the growing realization that the adolescent maturation of the brain's frontal lobes is far more important to human life than was previously known.

Although adolescence is a complex body/brain developmental phenomenon, it's useful to think of it as something that's especially focused in the maturation of our brain's frontal lobes, where we process conscious executive decisions about what to do and how to do it. Since frontal lobe researchers metaphorically compare the role and importance of our frontal lobes to a corporate CEO or a symphony conductor, adolescent frontal lobe maturation is something to be praised and not ridiculed as it fine-tunes itself into adult competence and autonomy. Autonomy doesn't emerge as easily as walking and talking. A sheltered childhood doesn't immediately translate into an independent, productive adulthood without a few exploratory mishaps along the way.

Only humans experience adolescence as an extended developmental stage, and scientists aren't sure why it should take us twice as long to mature as other primates with relatively long life spans. Cultural complexities drive much of our adolescent development, and most of the world's cultures are now very complex. Cultural complexity is a relatively recent development, however, and so what has occurred in the past several hundred years didn't affect human evolution. Regardless of the developmental reason, both parenting and schooling tend to shift into a different mode during adolescence—a shift away from the childhood focus on nurturing and sheltering toward a focus on at least recognizing, if not enhancing, the adolescent's inevitable reach for autonomy.

Our 20-year childhood and adolescence is actually advantageous, in that it allows us to master cultural knowledge through the extended observation of adult behavior that characterizes teaching and learning. The **mirror neuron** system and the plasticity capabilities inherent in our large **cerebral cortex** (both discussed in Chapter 2) provide the neurobiological foundation. (See the glossary, beginning on page 141, for definitions of **boldface terms**.) Parenting, schooling, and mass media provide the cultural context and the activation. Young people can thus concentrate their cognitive energies on cultural assimilation rather than on daily survival.

Geographers use an intriguing term, *adolescent stream*, to label a stream in transition in the erosion cycle. During this period, the weather and consequent water movement patterns sculpt the valley floor into what it will become. An *adolescent stream* is thus a meandering stream. It's a legitimate stream, but it's not yet what it will become.

A personal note: Like an *adolescent stream,* my wife and I meandered through our adolescence. The Introduction reported that we have seven children who also meandered through their adolescence into responsible adulthood. And we now have 20 grandchildren who are in various stages of meandering toward, through, or beyond adolescence. It was interesting to go through the experience firsthand, and then to observe two generations go through what is substantially the same experience—despite all the cultural changes that have occurred over the decades. So this book, which focuses principally on the organization, development, and nurturing of the brain that drives adolescence is based not only on the substantial emerging biological literature on adolescence but also on my extended personal experience as an adolescent, parent, grandparent, and educator.

adolescence is a work in progress [handwritten]

Immaturity of frontal lobe during adolescence can result in immature + inappropriate actions [handwritten]

Adolescent meandering implies that maturity often shifts our perspective of what constitutes appropriate behavior. An acquaintance once told me that he had gone to much effort and expense to construct a beautiful stained wooden fence that enclosed the part of his corner yard that adjoined the sidewalk. The morning following its completion, he discovered that someone—he assumed an adolescent—had used an aerosol paint can during the night to *tag* the outside length of the fence with crude words and designs. He was furious. And then he recalled that he and a friend had done something similar to someone's house when they were 16, and they thought it a funny prank. I expect that today's adolescent computer hackers will similarly resent the electronic destruction of their personal and business records by future adolescent hackers.

An adolescent with immature **frontal lobes** can thus be sufficiently mature to design and carry out a complex action, but not really realize until perhaps years later that the action was inappropriate and immature. Knowing how to do something isn't the same as knowing if you should do it. The development of the positive personal moral/ethical base that's characteristic of an autonomous adult is thus a central issue that this book will explore.

To help adolescents resolve such issues in an informed manner, the adults who nurture them should develop at least a functional understanding of the underlying neurobiology of adolescence. The adolescent brain, like an *adolescent stream*, is functionally a work in progress. So just as it's not a good idea to build a house on the continually shifting bank of an *adolescent stream*, it's inappropriate to expect functional stability in a developing adolescent brain. Confusion rather than consistency may often more accurately describe adolescent cognition and behavior—but don't think of adolescent confusion or adult cultural confusion about adolescence as something pejorative. Just as it's okay for a six-month-old to be unable to talk and walk, it's also okay for an adolescent to be unable to effectively carry out functions that will eventually mature, and it's also okay for our culture to not yet know how best to nurture adolescents in an era of rapid cultural change.

Although the cultural roles of children and adults are reasonably clear, we often send confusing and conflicting messages to adolescents about their expected cultural roles. We expect too little and too much. We expect adolescents to follow current cultural mores but to think for themselves. We deride their idealism as impractical but offer no successful alternatives to social issues. We finance their consumerism and then decry their wasteful behaviors. We laud virtuoso performance in adolescent sports and the arts, but we've reduced support for school physical education and arts programs. Adolescents are rapidly moving into adult body shapes, but we often (incorrectly) assume that their brain maturation is occurring at the same pace.

Our culture tends to have a confident sense of what's appropriate in the unequal adult/child and the egalitarian adult/adult relationships and responsibilities. We're less confident of what's appropriate in parental and parental surrogate/adolescent relationships and responsibilities. Let's briefly explore the cultural confusion that exists within adolescents and about adolescence as a prelude to a more extensive exploration of these issues in later chapters.

CONFUSION WITHIN ADOLESCENTS

I have a very clear recollection of my first substantial adolescent thoughts about my adult life. I was walking home from school in the spring of my 14th year thinking about my fall entrance into high school when it suddenly occurred to me that work and not play would dominate my adult life. I would soon have to get a job and assume responsibility for my personal and family life. I recall deciding during that walk home that I had better begin to think seriously about my vocational direction and then figure out how to become successful at it. I also started to think about my personal values and life in ways that I hadn't earlier. I suspect that you had a somewhat similar epiphany at about the same age—and that today's mid-teens are continuing the tradition. Goodbye, childhood.

[handwritten annotation in margin: shift in responsibility]

We adults tend to think of early adolescence as a mindless developmental period, but I believe that most contemporary adolescents contemplate adult life as thoughtfully as we did. It's just that they typically don't share such thoughts with adults as much as they do with the peers who will accompany them into adult life. Peers listen to vocational and other dreams without giving practical advice, and thus encourage imaginative mental exploration during a confusing transitional period. You and I did the same thing.

During my 14th summer, I got a job in a greenhouse, which I kept all through high school—and it sparked my lifelong fascination with biology. The owner, Nick Schroeder, was a fine mentor who took the time to explain why we did the things with plants that we did. Not surprisingly, I subsequently majored in biology in college, and again a favorite biology professor, Carl Brandhorst, became my mentor when I became his lab assistant. I loved and respected my parents, but these two nonparental mentors made a major impact on my adolescent life and adult vocation. Working together at a potting bench and assembling materials for a lab class sparked the kind of informal conversations about a range of issues that were emerging in my life. I didn't agree with everything my mentors told me—just as I didn't agree with everything my parents told me—but I thought about what they said.

Several colleagues recently recounted the similar range and importance of such adolescent mentoring in their lives—from their teachers, coaches, youth directors, bosses, adult coworkers, neighbors, uncles and aunts, grandparents. I didn't realize until years later that my father had quietly encouraged and expedited my greenhouse job in the hope that I would benefit from the mentoring that he believed I would get from Nick, a man he respected. I hope that similar nonparental mentors emerged during your adolescent years and will also emerge in the adolescents in your life.

The dramatic biological changes that occur during adolescence are another element that typically shifts an adolescent's self-concept and self-esteem, and can thus cause confusion. One of our sons grew several inches in a few months and suddenly drew the unwelcome interest of the school's basketball coach. Menarche biologically transforms a girl into a woman within 24 hours. Acne, whiskers, breasts, voice changes, body hair, shifts in sleeping patterns, erections at inopportune times, and a whole lot more all require understanding and patience as adolescents gradually become comfortable with their inevitable body transformations. They simultaneously want and don't want the attention of others. They frequently look in the mirror but often don't like what they see.

As adolescents shift loyalties from family to peer relationships, they increasingly compare themselves with others. They may not consciously realize it, but in doing this, they're beginning what will become adult competitions and collaborations for mates and resources. They often believe that friends and others have their act together more than they do (and of course, the others feel that way about them). This typical feeling of inadequacy may actually be positive if it it's kept in perspective, since it can encourage the sense of striving toward personal and social identity that's necessary for an autonomous adult life. When such comparisons and competitions get out of hand, they can cause all kinds of personal and social problems. Like seasonings, a little bit can help—a lot can hurt.

Style thus becomes important to adolescents—in clothing, language, music, behavior, and other elements of their social selves. Children are willing to follow parental direction on such decisions, but adolescents often use them as initial exploratory steps in designing their own individuality. They push to see how far they can go before their parents object. Tattoos and body piercing provide a currently popular search for limits. Mass media provide positive and negative role models on what to do and how to do it for unsure early adolescents who want to express their individuality, but within the constraints of what they consider acceptable to their peers.

Adolescents' seemingly fickle taste sometimes drives their parents to distraction. For example, a recently much desired and still perfectly good pair of shoes or other piece of apparel is suddenly no longer in style. Your adolescent desperately needs a replacement—and believes that *a loving parent* would instantly provide the funds. Strange as it seems, the initial adolescent reach for adult identity and autonomy is thus often embodied in a need to imitate what others are thinking and doing—and *others* typically doesn't include their parents.

CONFUSION ABOUT ADOLESCENTS

Adolescent changes sometimes seem to occur dramatically. A stranger suddenly seems to have entered our life. I've noticed such dramatic changes in adolescent grandchildren I hadn't seen for several months—the interim disappearance of the *child* look, the shift from conventional to unconventional behavior, the late-adolescent examples of unexpected and welcome maturity. Conversely, the same changes may emerge gradually and thus imperceptibly in the mind of an adult who constantly interacts with the adolescent. It's therefore helpful to develop a record of childhood and adolescence in a manner that psychologically helps to place immediate (and perhaps unsettling) experiences into the context of a more gradual (and hopefully positive) 20-year development. Computerized digital technologies now simplify this process.

For example, videotape your children for several minutes on each of their birthdays. Ask them to tell what they've done during the past year and to display and discuss objects of current importance to them. The film will eventually become a marvelous, hour-long record of a child's entire 20-year physical and psychological development. It can provide developmental context to a currently troubled adolescent, and it's perhaps also something to reassure you late at night while awaiting your adolescent's return home.

A teacher can similarly take several pictures of classroom life each day and select and digitally store the one that best characterized that day. On the final day of the year, project the entire sequence of pictures on a screen—a 45-minute roller-coaster ride through the school year that shows the class where they were at the beginning, what they've done during the school year, and what they've become at the end.

Adolescents are increasingly creating personal Web logs, or "blogs"—Internet diaries of their experiences and commentaries on their beliefs that they share electronically with friends. A blog is something like a computerized mirror that reflects a verbal picture of the blogger. And as with a diary, it's possible for adolescent bloggers to reread what they wrote months earlier—but also to compare their experiences with those of other adolescent bloggers. And being adolescents, they may also post things on the Internet that they wish they hadn't when they reach adult life and decide to run for public office.

Traditional beliefs about adolescence and artfully edited memories of our own adolescence cause some of our cultural confusion about adolescence. I'm sure that you quickly (and correctly) determined that my stories of a sudden 14-year-old realization of the reality of adult life and my subsequent after-school greenhouse job didn't tell the entire story of my adolescence. Adults are often caught between trying to recapture and recast the idyllic adolescence they now believe they had and shielding their own adolescents from any of their negative adolescent experiences.

My childhood occurred during the Great Depression of the 1930s, and most of my adolescence occurred during World War II. These were terribly distressing, historically significant periods, but many children today experience an analogous family financial devastation that occurs when seemingly secure parental jobs disappear—and war and the threat of terrorism seem a continuing reality. When generations compare their experiences, the old adage that the more things change, the more they remain the same holds true. Folks may like to think that they lived their early years in a more difficult time than their children and grandchildren, and that they behaved more appropriately—but I've lived long enough to doubt most of that rhetoric. Good and bad times and good and bad behavior are experienced individually and can occur anywhere and at any time. But having suggested that, it's also important to consider the problems our society currently confronts that make contemporary adolescence problematic in ways that differ significantly from earlier generations.

AN INTRODUCTION TO THE ISSUES
EXPLORED IN SUBSEQUENT CHAPTERS

Sexual maturation is a central element of adolescence, and adolescent sexual misbehavior has always occurred. However, sexual stimulation is much more available today via mass media than it's ever been. Furthermore, issues related to sexual orientation and sexually transmitted diseases similarly pose uniquely contemporary problems. Chapter 3 will focus on basic and contemporary issues of adolescent sexuality and bonding.

In simple societies, adolescents are a valuable family resource through their work in the family enterprise or through sharing their earnings with their family. Conversely, in more complex societies such as ours, adolescents become an increasingly significant financial burden on a family. I wrote above about getting a stimulating afterschool job at 14—something that's not as easy for today's adolescents. Adolescent requests for money, coupled with their grousing about helping to maintain the family housing (let alone their own room and possessions, for goodness sake), simply add to parental irritation. When adolescents are at their worst, it's difficult to imagine the adult reciprocal companionship and support most parents will eventually get from them. Chapter 4 will focus on basic and contemporary issues of adolescent productivity and their search for a vocation.

Our increasingly electronic society has created many moral and ethical issues that center on adolescents, such as downloading copyrighted materials, assembling term papers from Internet sources, and a whole lot more. Chapters 5 and 7 will focus on basic and contemporary issues related to the development of a moral and ethical sense in adolescents.

The lure of challenge and a tendency toward risk taking characterize adolescence. Body capabilities and curiosity develop before judgment. Disability and death are serious adolescent problems, exacerbated by increasingly powerful automobiles and other motorized vehicles. Chapter 6 will focus on basic and contemporary issues related to adolescent risk and security.

Adolescence is a major developmental period, but we humans always seek to go beyond our cognitive and motor capabilities via the technologies we develop, and to medicate ourselves into abnormal states with drugs. Drugs are an especially problematic issue in adolescence because of body/brain chemical shifts that occur during adolescence. Chapter 7 will focus on basic and contemporary issues related to adolescent use of technology—and drugs are a form of technology.

Each generation seems to create its own stories and art forms, and music and body adornment are especially important elements of adolescent life. Adults typically are appalled by adolescent music and body art. Chapter 8 will focus on basic and contemporary issues related to adolescence and the arts and humanities.

Finally, adolescents continuously search for and evaluate potential partners who will accompany them into adult life. Adolescents are reaching for personal autonomy, but they want friends to be with them when they attain it. Autonomy is a somewhat nebulous concept about becoming successfully self-directed within cultural constraints. Chapter 9 will focus on basic and contemporary issues related to the adolescent search for peer collaborators and their concomitant reach for autonomy.

Adolescence is typically an optimistic period in one's life. No other decade is quite like it. Adults tend to look askance at adolescents, but the truth is that adolescents are as fascinating and enjoyable as they are incomprehensible and distressing— often more so. The chapters that follow will explore adolescence within the context of that positive/negative mix.

The exploration will begin in Chapter 2 with a nontechnical explanation of the organization and development of the human brain, the best-organized, most functional three pounds of matter in the known universe. Awesomely complex biologically but also elegantly simple functionally, it's responsible for Beethoven's Ninth Symphony, computers, the Sistine

Chapel, automobiles, the Second World War, Hamlet, apple pie—and adolescence.

And especially adolescence, since that's when our basic cognitive development just about concludes, maturation just about emerges, and adult life really begins to loom.

It's important for parents, educators, and other adults to realize that our brain's complexity and adaptability allow us to live successfully within a wide variety of environments and cultures. No single recipe for human success exists. And although it's also true that no single recipe exists for rearing and educating a young person, a couple of important general nurturing principles grounded in the organization and development of our brain should guide parents and educators—and so they'll be explored further throughout this book:

1. Children are born helpless and so have a birthright to a safe and healthy environment and to unconditional love—to be loved for who they are rather than for what they do. We adults seem to provide unconditional love more easily when an infant messes up a diaper than when an adolescent messes up a car, when a primary student misspells a word than when an adolescent student misplaces homework.

Most children soon discover the reality of rewards and punishments—that adults often conditionally (rather than unconditionally) dispense acceptance and love as a reward for satisfactory behavior. By adolescence, many young people have thus learned to focus more on satisfying the desires of others than on developing their own personal interests and the collaborative skills that adult autonomy and a democratic society require. A custodial policy based on rewards and punishments may thus have short-term benefits in the efficient operation of a family and school, but it may also delay the development of autonomy.

Conditional love is often, and unfortunately, a two-way street. Infants do love unconditionally, but childhood begins the litany of demands and of punishing misbehavior if parents don't instantly respond. And so the battle over control and autonomy begins early, and adolescence often escalates it.

2. Young people will also learn how the natural and cultural worlds work during their 20-year development and that their behavior has natural consequences. For example, equipment broken by misuse doesn't operate; a stated unkind comment can't be deleted. But they'll also learn that adults will often inappropriately ascribe unrelated negative natural consequences to behavior. "If you don't clean up your room immediately, you can't watch TV this evening." Such statements simply confuse young people, who correctly perceive no natural rational relationship between the organization (or disorganization) of their bedroom and watching TV in the living room. Such adult rhetoric thus delays the development of a clear differentiation between natural and contrived consequences and so also the development of adult autonomy.

[handwritten margin note: lack of natural relationship between actions + consequences → creates]

Worse, such rhetoric can come back to haunt us: "If I can't go to Mary's party just because her parents won't be home, no one will ever talk to me again!" Now, where do adolescents learn that kind of skewed logic?

The natural consequences of this situation above might be to remind the adolescent that all who share a home must help maintain the public and private areas. An adolescent who chooses to not maintain personal space (one's room) can thus be evicted from that space or be required to maintain a greater-than-equal share of the public space (such as the living room or yard), but not participating in maintaining the home isn't an option.

Our brain is organized to receive, integrate, interpret, and respond to the environmental messages it receives from the natural and cultural worlds it inhabits; and it can also imagine an environment that doesn't currently exist and then act on it. To understand adolescence, we therefore must understand our brain.

CHAPTER TWO

Brain Organization and Development

Being Human

The planning, regulation, and prediction of movements are the principal reasons for a brain. Plants are as biologically successful as animals, but they don't have brains. An organism that's not going anywhere of its own volition doesn't need a brain. It doesn't even need to know where it is. What's the point? Being an immobile plant does have its advantages, however. Plants don't have to get up every day and go to work, because they're already there.

On the other hand, if an organism has legs, wings, or fins, it needs a sensory system that will inform it about here and there, a make-up-its-mind system to determine whether here is better than there or there is better than here, and a motor system to get it to there if that's the better choice—as it is, alas, when we have to go to work.

Human movement isn't limited to the physical movements of our leg/foot/toe system. We can also use our arm/hand/finger system to grasp and throw, and our neck/face/mouth system to rhythmically activate the stream of air molecules that will move thoughts from our brain into the ears and brains of others. So speech and song are also forms of human movement. The arts add aesthetic qualities to mobility by encouraging us to move with style and grace: to dance and prance, to sculpt and strum, to play a trumpet and trumpet a play. Chapter 8 will further discuss this phenomenon.

We also move psychologically, such as when adolescents leave childhood and reach for adult autonomy, move from being single into bonded relationships, and move from being unemployed to employed. We've also added and improved on many technological extensions to supplement the limitations of biological movement—from wagons to automobiles, ladders to escalators, mail to e-mail, and spears to guns.

So to be human is to move in many different ways—from the ritual movements associated with conception at the beginning of life to those associated with burial at the end. Further, individual and mass movements are central to the history of most religious and cultural groups. The Biblical departure from the Garden of Eden and the Jewish Exodus from Egypt, Mohammed's journey from Mecca to Medina, and the Mormon trek to Utah are notable examples, but so are *The Odyssey*, *Moby Dick*, the Lewis and Clark Expedition, and every journey through adolescence.

Movement occurs internally as well as externally. Our heart beats and our lungs expand and contract. Blood and nutrients flow through our circulatory system. Food moves through our 30-foot-long digestive tube. **Neurotransmitters** move across the synaptic gap. Viral and bacterial invaders move throughout our body. Hair and nails extend. What's amazing is that our brain regulates all such internal and external movements and predicts and responds to the movements of others and objects. When movement stops, we die.

Mirror Neurons

But how do we initially activate and then master specific, conscious movements? The recent dramatic discovery of the mirror neuron system explains key elements of the process. Mirror neurons in our brain's motor regulation regions prime nearby motor neurons to activate sequentially when we carry out a conscious movement (such as a smile or a handshake)— but they also activate when we observe another person carry out that action. In effect, they create a mental template within our brain of the related neural activity that's occurring within the brain of the person we're observing.

The development of a smoothly controlled motor system is a major childhood priority, and it must begin to develop in infancy without much formal instruction. Therefore, if you stick out your tongue at an observant infant shortly after birth, the probability is high that she will reciprocate the behavior, because her mirror neurons will sequentially activate the motor neurons that then project her tongue. If we adults see someone yawning, we similarly experience the impetus to yawn. We may stifle the yawn, but infants who have to master many movements typically mimic anything they observe. Baby see, baby do.

Mirror neurons won't respond to the mere observation of a leg, hand, or mouth—except when it's carrying out a goal-directed action. Further, they will respond to a hand, but not to a tool, that's grasping or moving an object—since body movement systems, and not tools, are represented in our motor areas.

Mirror neurons thus facilitate the preliminary simulation, priming, programming, and rehearsing of motor neurons that occur throughout life, and this process obviously enhances our eventual mastery of complex motor behaviors and, as suggested above, our ability to *read* the minds of others—to predict movements. For example, inferring the potential movements of others is essential in avoiding approaching pedestrians, in the complementary movements of dance partners, and in *faking out* opponents in many games. Mirror neuron simulation may also explain why so many people enjoy observing virtuoso athletes, dancers, and musicians. It allows us to mentally represent masterful movements that we can't physically mimic. Note the body language of former athletes observing a game as they mimic the actions of the athletes.

Scientists are also exploring the relationship between mirror neuron activity and our ability to imagine our own planned actions, be empathetic, and develop articulate speech merely by hearing it. A preliterate child's mirror neuron system seemingly activates the same speech mechanisms that the speaker activates. Speech involves very complex movements, and so initially, infants can only babble within a verbal environment, but they eventually develop articulate speech.

When we observe someone in the initial stages of a movement sequence, such as when a diner picks up a knife and fork, we can usually infer the subsequent actions because our brain is *mirroring* the movement sequence and so *knows* what will occur next. When a speaker stops in midsentence, we can often complete the sentence.

Mirror neurons will probably help to explain many teaching and learning mysteries, in which modeling provides young people with an effective behavioral pattern to follow—and may help to explain disabilities—such as autism—in which children can't *read* the minds of others or speak effectively.

Adolescents spend much of their time observing and mimicking the movements of others, so it's like starting anew. In infancy, they mirrored the movements of their parents, who introduced them to human life, and now in adolescence they mirror the movements of their peers, who will accompany them into adult life.

Our search for the meaning and nurturing of adolescence must therefore begin with the organization and extended development of the maturing brain that regulates our decade-long, sometimes awkward, but always fascinating journey through adolescence. When adolescents aren't asleep, they're typically on the go—even when they're not sure of the destination.

This chapter provides nontechnical functional and anatomical explanations of our brain's organization and development, with a special focus on those elements that help to define adolescence. Appendixes toward the back of the book contain more technical explanations of selected elements for those who wish to learn more, and the glossary defines unfamiliar terms that you may confront at various points in the book. An annotated list of current print and electronic resources will allow you to go beyond the confines of this book.

THE ORGANIZATION OF THE HUMAN BRAIN

Brain Cells

The numbers are immense, and the movement of information is constant. Our brain is composed of perhaps 100 billion neurons and a trillion **glial cells**. Neurons, functioning within massive, highly interconnected networks, receive and send specific information that's coded into the chemistry of more than 50 different types of specialized neurotransmitter molecules. Glial cells provide a variety of structural and processing support services.

Our brain seems incomprehensible at the cellular level, and in some respects, it is. Scientists have a better understanding of how brain cells function than of why they function collaboratively as they do to regulate body processes and to interact with a very complex and ambiguous world.

Neurons are cells, just like the other 100 trillion cells in our body, but they differ significantly in form and function. All body cells have (1) an outer semipermeable membrane that encapsulates jellylike nutrient material (cytoplasm) and contains channels for the selective input and output of nutrients and cell products; and (2) various processing and regulatory structures—principally, a nucleus that contains the cell's long, coiled, tightly packed **deoxyribonucleic acid (DNA)** molecule—that provide the genetic directions for protein synthesis.

Since the function of neurons is to move information throughout our brain and body (via neurotransmitter molecules), they also contain tubular **dendrite** and **axon** extensions that connect the neuron with other cells. Dendrites are short cellular extensions that receive chemical information from other neurons and sense organs. A neuron's axon is typically a single longer, branched extension that sends electrochemical information to other neurons and muscles. A single neuron can be connected to thousands of other neurons and sensory/glandular/motor cells at various distances.

Figure 2.1 shows a functional model of two related neurons. Appendix A provides a more complete explanation of

Figure 2.1   A Functional Model of Two Related Neurons

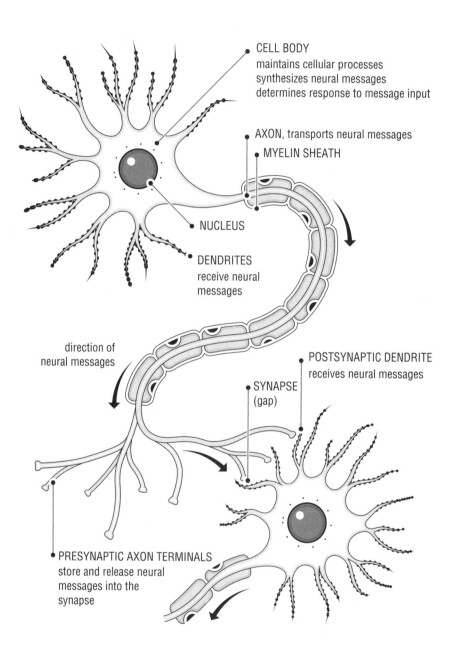

how neurons and neurotransmitters process information, and Chapter 7 will discuss the relationship between neurotransmitters and drugs.

Brain Systems: Functional

Our brain is basically a social system. Even a simple task requires the collaboration of many systems and subsystems. For example, separate subsystems within our visual system process quantity, color, shape, location, and movement. Their collaborative activity can lead to the integrated perception of two red balls rolling across a table—which may spark our brain's decision-making systems to pick up the closer ball and our arm/hand/finger motor systems to carry out the action. (1)

[handwritten margin notes: order of brain development; (1) Systems for survival; (2) Systems for qualitative social life]

Our brain's early development focuses on the genetically driven, species-specific processing systems that are necessary for survival. Later development focuses on the environmentally driven, culturally specific processing systems that are necessary for a qualitative social life. For example, our ability to speak is innate, but learning to speak a specific language is culturally specific. Most adolescent learning is culturally specific.

We're born with a basic, survival-level version of most brain systems, and they develop and function at that level with limited instruction and effort. Explicit instruction and extended practice mature such systems so that they can respond to more complex, culturally driven challenges. A normal human ability range exists that limits response beyond this range to virtuosos and savants—and to the technologies that we develop to extend performance of the function beyond our biological capabilities. Speaking is thus innate, reading must be explicitly taught, and writing requires a tool such as a pencil or a computer. Similarly, walking is innate, tap dancing must be explicitly taught, and wheels and wings extend the distance and speed of human movement.

Our brain's hundreds of cognitive systems don't mature simultaneously. Children can thus grasp the rolling red ball in the example above before they can walk across the room to get it. The sequential maturation of various brain systems is a central issue in understanding adolescence, since several brain systems that are critically important to autonomous adult life don't mature until upper adolescence. The systems that regulate moral and ethical judgment are perhaps the most noteworthy examples.

Two central tasks confront us: stay alive and get into the gene pool. To do this, we must have brain systems that are functionally organized to effectively *recognize* and *respond* to *novel* and *familiar dangers* and *opportunities* related to such survival needs as food, shelter, and mating. Major brain systems are dedicated to each of these three pairs of cognitive concepts.

Recognizing and responding to challenges typically follows a three-stage sequence:

- *Engagement.* Important internal and external sensory information or our internal imagination activates our arousal/alerting system (emotion), which activates our focusing system (attention).
- *Solution and Decision.* Emotional arousal and attentional focusing activate our various solution and decision-making systems (learning/memory, reason/logic, problem solving).
- *Action.* A decision activates our motor response systems (behavior, movement).

These systems may not function smoothly during adolescence, so adolescents may over- or underrespond to emotional stimuli, or respond impetuously rather than consider rational alternatives. Subsequent chapters will explain such dysfunctional behavior.

Brain Systems: Anatomical

Our brain is anatomically organized and develops from bottom to top, back to front, and right to left. Figure 2.2 presents a stylized perspective.

Figure 2.2   Stylized View of Brain Functions

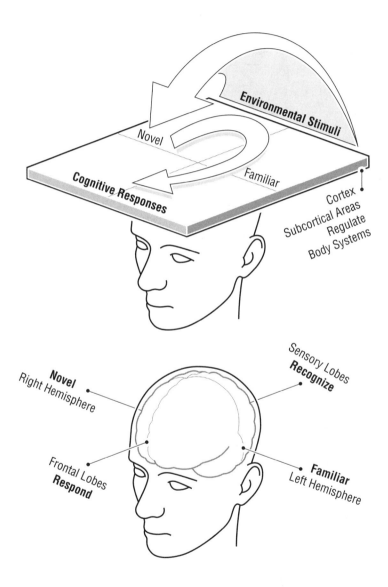

Bottom-to-Top Organization

Our brain is composed of (1) **subcortical systems** in and around our finger-size **brain stem** that subconsciously and reflexively regulate such survival functions as respiration and circulation, and synthesize and distribute many of the neurotransmitters that move chemical information within and among neural networks; (2) a **cerebellum** (located behind the brain stem) that coordinates fine movement sequences with sensory information and participates with the frontal lobes in complex planning activities; and (3) a large, overlying, six-layer, deeply folded sheet of **cerebral cortex** (or simply **cortex**) that consciously and reflectively processes learned information and behaviors. The cerebral cortex (which is about the area and thickness of a stack of six 12 × 18-inch sheets of construction paper) encompasses about 80 percent of the mass of our brain. Figure 2.3 shows an internal view of our brain and selected systems. Appendix B describes the organization of the cortex in more detail.

It may seem strange that such a small subcortical part of our brain regulates so many body systems, but body functions such as circulation and respiration are repetitive rather than complex, and so the system must only establish and maintain a constant rhythmic pattern. Conversely, the cortex must recognize and respond to many complex, ambiguous, and irregular challenges, and so it requires much more neuronal processing capability.

Since our immediate environment is rich in dangers and opportunities that range widely in importance, our brain's (principally subconscious and subcortical) emotional arousal system functions somewhat as a biological thermostat that determines when a specific environmental change reaches the threshold of being sufficiently important to activate the several (principally conscious and **cortical**) systems that focus attention and develop appropriate responses. For example, our emotional system will alert our attention, recognition, and response systems to the rapid approach of something very large. These cortical systems will recognize it as a car and

Figure 2.3   Selected Interior Brain Systems

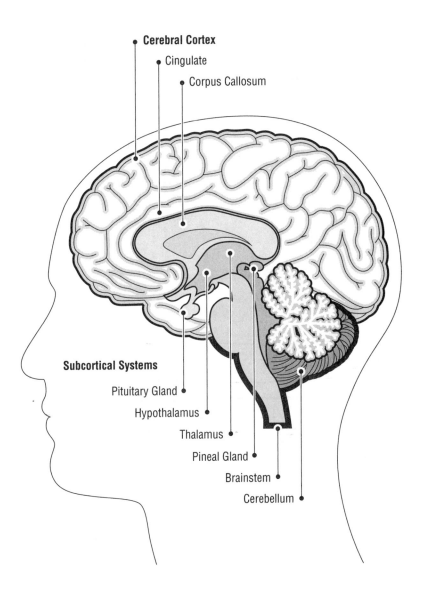

activate an appropriate avoidance behavior. So even if the subcortical areas of our brain are relatively small, they power-fully regulate circulation, respiration, emotional arousal, and a number of other survival functions.

Of necessity, our subconscious emotional system matures early, but our conscious problem-solving systems mature during adolescence. The adolescent coordination of emotional arousal with rational thought is thus often problematic during its extended maturation.

Back-to-Front Organization of the Cortex

Imagine a line across your skull from ear to ear. Each of the cerebral **hemispheres** contains an **occipital** (vision), **parietal** (touch), and **temporal** (hearing) sensory **lobe** located in the rear section, and a frontal lobe in the front section, as illus-trated in Figure 2.4. The paired sensory lobes are specialized to recognize and accurately interpret the dynamics of the cur-rent challenge, and the frontal lobes are specialized to use that information to determine and execute an appropriate response. The back-to-front organization of our cortex is thus an inte-grated recognition/response system.

Incoming sensory information is initially processed toward the back of the sensory lobes. It then moves forward within the sensory lobes, where it is integrated into a perceptual (recog-nition) model of the external environment. Recall the percep-tion of two red balls rolling across a table that emerged out of the integration of specific quantity, color, shape, movement, and location sensory subsystems. Separate pathways focus on the identification and location of the various elements of the challenge.

The principal maturation of the frontal lobes (comprising about a third of the cerebral cortex) occurs during adolescence. As suggested above, our survival is dependent on our ability to effectively recognize and respond to the novel and familiar dangers and opportunities we confront. Our frontal lobes allow us to move from the purely reactive behavior of most animals

Figure 2.4   Major Cerebral Cortex Regions

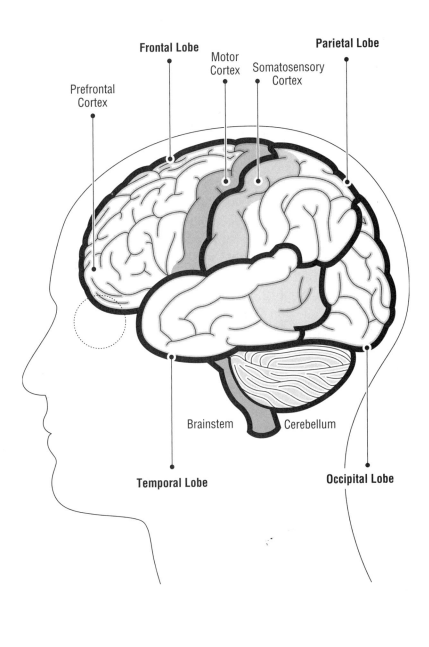

to being principally proactive, capable of consciously antici-
pating and preparing for potential novel and familiar
challenges. They thus allow us to consider options, predict
consequences, and properly pace the elements of our response.

The **prefrontal cortex** area (directly behind our forehead)
is directly interconnected with every distinct functional unit
of our brain, and so it coordinates and integrates most brain
functions—and is the principal repository of the general goals
that affect our decisions. Like an efficient computer search
engine, it can quickly locate information necessary to make
such decisions. Problem solving and decision making thus
begin at the level of a general goal that becomes more specific
as the processing activity moves backward to the **motor cortex**, where conscious responses are initiated.

Separate pathways process the cognitive issues of how
and whether to respond to the challenge. It should come as no
surprise to discover that the _how-to-do-it_ capabilities mature
before the _whether-to-do-it_ capabilities. Therefore, many adolescents can successfully do things that they shouldn't.

We're a social species, and so much of our cognitive strength
comes from our ability to successfully understand and interact
with others. Frontal lobe systems (such as the **anterior cingulate**, **orbitofrontal cortex**, and mirror neurons) play key roles in
developing and regulating social awareness and behavior. Early
social stimulation is thus as important to the later maturation of
our frontal lobes as early sensory stimulation is to the development of our sensory lobes and perceptual processes.

The importance of effective frontal lobes is further under-
scored by the growing awareness that many mental disorders
(from attention deficits to schizophrenia) are associated principally with frontal lobe malfunctions.

Our sensory lobes thus play a major role in developing
mental models of the external world. Our frontal lobes manipulate and transform these models in a variety of ways—such
as when we develop tools and procedures that carry out a
function that our body and brain alone can't accomplish at the
levels we seek. We can thus consider much of technology as
an extension of our sensory and frontal lobes—providing us

Many mental
disabilities are
associated w/
frontal lobe
malfunctions

with distinct additional advantages as we intelligently recognize and respond to current and potential dangers and opportunities. Chapter 7 will discuss this in more detail.

Right-to-Left Organization of the Cortex

The cortex is also divided into right and left hemispheres. The fundamental organizing principle for the right and left hemispheres emerges out of an important question a brain must ask whenever danger or opportunity looms: Have I confronted this challenge before?

The right hemisphere (in most humans) is organized principally to process novel challenges and creative solutions, and the left hemisphere familiar challenges and established routines. For example, we process strange faces principally in our right hemisphere, and familiar faces in our left. Musically naïve people process music principally in the right hemisphere; trained musicians, in the left.

Although both hemispheres are active in processing most cognitive functions, the relative level of involvement shifts from the right to the left hemisphere over time and with increased familiarity and competence. The exploratory right hemisphere is thus organized to respond rapidly and creatively to a novel challenge, but the more stable processing systems in the left hemisphere eventually transform the successful initial responses into an efficient, established routine that we activate whenever the challenge recurs.

This makes sense. Grammatical language is an efficient, established procedure to enhance communication within a socially complex species, so it's not surprising that considerable left hemisphere space is devoted to it. Dependent infants use whatever nonverbal communication skills they can creatively muster to get needed help, but they then happily spend much of their childhood mastering the much more efficient existing cultural language template that we pass from generation to generation.

Similarly, children don't have to create personal routines for many other cognitive functions—from tying shoes to flying kites. We teach them how to do it. There's no inherent logic to the order of the letters of the alphabet, but it makes sense—for data classification purposes—for everyone to use the same sequence, so preschool children learn the alphabet song long before they need to use a dictionary.

Learning thus typically begins with right hemisphere exploration, something often ignored in schools that teach students the answers to questions they didn't ask. Students thus learn the answer but don't really understand the question or challenge it. What's the point of mastering an established algorithm or other cognitive routine if the child or adolescent hasn't yet confronted an appropriate precursor of the adult challenge, and so doesn't know when to activate the learned routine?

A young child enjoys learning the alphabet song and all the attention its successful mastery brings. That the sequence has social utility is a serendipity discovered later. But what about learning how to divide 4,723 by 69 when it's difficult for a developing right hemisphere to even imagine the problem in real life? What about memorizing factual information of historical events that have no immediate or potential personal meaning? The continuing parental/school challenge is to create an appropriate mix of exploratory and didactic instruction.

It's obviously important to master efficient, culturally important routines, but left hemisphere routines are best developed through right hemisphere explorations focused initially on understanding the nature and importance of the challenge.

What occurs within the various processing systems of one brain that's confronting a novel challenge has an intriguing parallel within a group of brains. Imagine a committee charged with resolving a novel organizational challenge. The members must determine its dynamics and then agree on a solution. We typically use the term *brainstorming* to describe what they initially do, and it's akin to what occurs within our right hemisphere's sensory/frontal lobe processing systems.

All ideas are initially acceptable in brainstorming, but the discussion will eventually converge on a smaller number of viable explanations and proposals, and finally on a decision.

We teach students answers to ?'s never asked

It doesn't necessarily have to be the best decision, just something workable that can achieve consensus. The discussion and decision are then recorded in the minutes (or by extension, stored in our brain's and/or computer's memory system).

When a similar problem emerges later, the record is retrieved and edited to meet any different circumstances, and those decisions are then saved. This process continues until the committee creates a policy that it will automatically follow whenever this problem or a close variant occurs.

Think about your own thought processes when confronting a novel challenge, and you can almost sense your brain's various processing systems *brainstorming* as they try to make up their collective mind.

Adolescents spend much time and energy in brainstorming activities—seemingly endless discussions with friends about what to do and how to do it. Adults tend to deride this, but such social exploration helps to develop the cognitive and negotiation skills they'll use later in more important personal and corporate problem-solving activities.

It's efficient for individuals and organizations to develop effective routines for familiar recurring problems. The comprehension and creative resolution of a novel challenge require much more time and energy, even though the process is intellectually stimulating. As we age, we therefore tend to develop an increasingly large repertoire of routines that we incorporate into the resolution of a wide variety of challenges. We may come to resent novel challenges because we lack the considerable energy they require. We thus become *set in our ways.*

The arts and sports have been historically important in all cultures, and their principal purpose may be to exercise body and mind. Their inherent novel challenges spark right hemisphere explorations in informal, nonthreatening settings, so that we'll be in physical and cognitive shape to tackle analogous real-life problems when they occur. Adolescents certainly spend much of their time and energy on play and game activities that prepare them for adult challenges. Chapters 6 and 8 discuss this issue further.

THE DEVELOPMENT OF THE HUMAN BRAIN

We're born with a very immature brain (about a third of its adult size) because of our mothers' upright stance and consequent relatively narrow birth canal. Our helpless beginning and long juvenile dependency prompted us to become a cooperative social species with a rich, language-driven culture.

Social skills are thus developmentally important—and in our complex society, it's very important that immature children learn how to communicate and collaborate effectively with those who aren't kin, and who don't even share the values and traditions that are important to one's supportive family.

We can divide our 20-year developmental trajectory into two periods of approximately 10 years. The childhood developmental period from birth to about age 10 focuses on learning how to be *a human being*—learning to move, to communicate, and to master basic cultural knowledge and social skills. The adolescent developmental period (from 11 to 20+) focuses on learning how to be *a productive reproductive human being*—planning for a vocation, exploring emotional commitment and sexuality, developing a moral and ethical base, and reaching for adult autonomy.

The first four years of each of these two decade-long developmental periods are characterized by slow, awkward beginnings prior to a normal six-year move toward confidence and competence. For example, crawling leads to toddling leads to walking leads to running and leaping and dancing.

We can thus think of the preschool years as the awkward years and the K–5 school years as the move toward confident competence in childhood sensory lobe maturation. We can similarly think of the middle school years as the awkward years and the high school/college years as the move toward confidence competence in adolescent frontal lobe maturation. These decade-long developmental periods are characterized principally by the increased efficiency of connections among neural networks and the elimination of unneeded connections.

We tend to be far more indulgent of the inevitable developmental awkwardness and errors of preschool children than of the related awkwardness and errors of early adolescents in their middle school years. Demanding adults tend to forget that the mastery of something as complex as reflective thought or one's sexuality didn't occur instantly and without error in their lives, and it likewise probably won't in their adolescent's life.

Competence during the first 10 years is characterized by a move toward rapid automatic responses to challenges. For example, slow, laborious initial reading tends to become reasonably automatic by age 10. Spelling, numerical computation, and the recall of cultural facts follow a similar trajectory.

Language includes the automatic mastery of a verbal taxonomy of generally accepted object, action, quality, and relationship categories. Similarly, morality and ethics include the mastery of a social taxonomy of culturally acceptable behaviors.

Competence during the second 10 years, however, is often appropriately characterized by delayed and reflective responses processed principally in the frontal lobes. For example, the common impulsive, instant-gratification responses of a child become less impulsive as a maturing adolescent learns to explore options and social implications prior to making a response.

Let's place this emerging adolescent competence into a biological context. We have two separate solution/response systems:

1. Challenges with a sense of immediacy are rapidly and reflexively processed by our brain's innate stress-driven, conceptual (principally subcortical) problem-solving system. This system responds quickly on the basis of a small amount of emotionally intense information. It's thus quite vulnerable to making racist/sexist/elitist responses that focus on only a few highly observable, emotion-charged elements.

2. Challenges without a sense of immediacy are processed more slowly and reflectively by our brain's curiosity-driven, analytical, principally cortical, problem-solving system.

We thus will respond *reflexively* to a car moving swiftly toward us (concerned only with its looming rapid approach), but we'll generally respond *reflectively* to a car on a sales lot, if we're considering its purchase (and are thus concerned with its service history, possible malfunctioning systems, cost, and so on).

Our rapid reflexive system is the default system because it responds to dangers and opportunities that require an immediate, decisive, fight-or-flight response that will enhance survival. When it isn't immediately obvious whether a reflexive or reflective response is the more appropriate, both systems simultaneously search for a solution, with the reflexive system typically responding first.

Most of us thus go through life with a long string of regrets and apologies because of the late arrival of our brain's (often better) reflective response. Since many problems humans now face don't require an impulsively reflexive response, the challenge is to help young people develop and use their frontal lobe capabilities in a low-threat reflective environment.

Marketing directed at young people—and at adults, for that matter—frequently seeks to activate reflexive rather than reflective responses. Elements such as bright colors, rapid movement, and oscillating sound are combined to enhance a product's sense of importance, and thus trigger a rapid purchase response.

Adolescent Frontal Lobe Maturation

As indicated above, the sensory lobes (which recognize and analyze challenges) mature during childhood, and the frontal lobes (which determine an appropriate response) mature during adolescence and early adulthood. Since our frontal lobes provide the solutions we need to survive, one might think that they should mature first—but then we would be solving problems that we don't understand—and we can all think of the effects of personal, government, and business decisions that were made without a clear understanding of the problem.

The cultural strategy for dealing with children with immature frontal lobes is to expect the adults in their lives to make major frontal lobe decisions for them—where to live, what to wear, when to go to bed, and so on. When children do make decisions, an adult is usually nearby to veto it if it's inappropriate. If no adult is nearby, children will typically do what they think an adult would do in that situation—and they usually know, since they spend a lot of time observing adults making such decisions. And as indicated earlier, we teach children how to make the important decisions they need to make—how to cross a street or ride a bus, how to use a phone to call for help, and how to identify and respond to potential predators.

Children with immature frontal lobes are willing to let adults make many decisions for them. Infants who can't walk are similarly willing to let adults carry them. But just as young children generally don't want to be carried while they're learning to walk, adolescents don't want adults to make frontal lobe decisions for them while their frontal lobes are maturing.

The only way we can learn to walk is to practice walking, and the only way we can mature our frontal lobes is to practice the reflective problem solving and advanced social skills that our frontal lobes process—even though young people aren't very successful with it initially. Adolescence thus becomes a challenge for adolescents and also for the significant adults in their life.

Here's the problem: If a toddler falls down, the damage is usually minor. But an adolescent's awkwardness or bad decision can lead to something far more serious—an auto accident, or a pregnancy. As the potential for damage increases, the concern of the adults in an adolescent's life also increases.

The importance of extracurricular activities in a typical adolescent's school experience is centered in the many opportunities a wise selection of such activities provides for the development of autonomous decision making in a relatively safe and nonthreatening setting, with limited adult interference. Similarly, adolescents spend a lot of time simply *hanging out* with each other. They sense the need to distance themselves from their adult relatives in order to learn how to live with their peers, who will become integral to their adult lives. They basically all mature together.

The constant peer conversations and planning of events that don't ever reach fruition thus enhance the maturation of all their frontal lobes. We could facetiously suggest that a group of conversing adolescents might have enough functioning frontal lobe neurons among them to make up one complete set of functioning frontal lobes, but it's important to realize that they're heavily involved in the adolescent equivalent of moving from crawling to toddling to walking to running and jumping and dancing.

Schools tend to limit the time adolescent students have to complete a task. It's probably better for frontal lobe maturation to restrict space. For example, give students whatever time they need to complete the project, but require them to reduce the final report to a page or so, or a minute or two. This requires them not only to explore everything but also to get to the heart of the issue in their report—to edit out all extraneous information that merely pads the document or presentation. Adult life often requires reflective summary judgments, such as in the development of a résumé, grant proposal, or project report. Success in many vocations (from mechanics to medicine) similarly depends on the accurate diagnosis and synthesis of the problem.

MAINTAINING A DEVELOPING BRAIN

Our brain accounts for only 2 percent of our body's weight, but it uses 20 percent of our body's energy. Nutrition and rest are thus as important to the development and maintenance of a brain as the various forms of cognitive stimulation and exercise that develop effective body/brain systems.

Food

Children are often picky eaters who dislike foods (such as cauliflower, carrots, and broccoli) that they later enjoy as adults. Since plants can't run away from predators, they develop toxins in such key structures as stems and roots to discourage herbivore nibbling. These toxins especially affect rapidly developing tissue, and since children are growing rapidly, they often respond negatively to the mild plant toxins that grown-up adults find piquant.

Adolescence typically changes eating patterns. The adolescent growth spurt can turn formerly picky eaters into voracious eaters. Eating disorders such as anorexia and bulimia also tend to begin in adolescence—and other adolescents suffer from obesity. Fast food and junk food with questionable nutritional value have become integral to adolescent culture. Afterschool extracurricular programs tend to negatively affect opportunities for family dinners. Eating thus becomes yet another area of adolescent life that slides away from parental influence—and unfortunately at a time when a proper diet is especially important.

It's best to develop good eating habits in young people from infancy on. Good nutrition flows from a situation in which meals are celebratory family events that frequently involve children in food preparation and presentation. We won't turn up our nose at something we helped to prepare. Family gardening and shopping at farmers' markets and pick-your-own farms add to the development of an organic sense that food isn't something that arrives only in *just-add-water-and-heat* packaging.

Make nutritious versions of such fast-food favorites as pizza, pasta, hamburgers, tacos, and fried chicken. Conceal disliked vegetables in salsa, guacamole, and blended soups. Teach your children how to bake nutritious bread and cookies.

Make nutritious snacks to eat while watching films and TV. It's perhaps easier to purchase ready-made food, but involving children in preparation pays huge dividends in how they perceive food.

Rest

We sleep away about one third of our life—in four to six, approximately 90-minute sleeping/dreaming cycles a night. The purpose of sleeping and dreaming still isn't clear. It's important to detour the traffic off a road that's being repaired, and it's similarly important to shut down interference from our sensorimotor systems while our brain carries out necessary maintenance tasks and the consolidation of memories that scientists believe occurs during sleeping and dreaming

Children and adolescents should get 9 hours of sleep a night, but apparently only about 20 percent of adolescents get that much. Further, many adolescents psychologically move two times zones west of where they live—falling asleep and waking later than they did as children. School schedules typically force them into an unfortunate variant of jet lag, and almost a third report dozing off in school at least once a week.

Glycogen, found in glial support cells, is a molecule that especially interests sleep researchers. It's the stored form of glucose, the brain's energy source. Like gasoline in a car, glycogen stores are depleted by activity and so must be replenished during inactive periods, such as sleep or naps, during which sensorimotor activity is inhibited. The complex chemical-replenishing process requires periods of brain activity but not wakefulness, and this may help to explain the nature of periodic dream sleep throughout the night, during which our brain activity resembles that of an awake brain.

Scientists have noted increased activity in brain areas that process vision and emotion during dreaming and decreased activity in areas that process rational thought and attention. This tends to concur with the emotional, visual, irrational, distorted content of dreams. Our 2 hours of nightly dreaming may thus give our normally rational brain an opportunity to imagine and test solutions to life's problems without being inhibited by rational thought, and this unconscious exploration may enhance subsequent conscious creativity.

Sleeping and dreaming may also play an ill-understood role in the consolidation, editing, and erasing of memories, especially procedural or skill memories. Memory formation and editing involve synaptic alterations in the neural networks involved in processing a memory, and such alterations are more easily effected during periods in which a brain isn't consciously active in thought and behavior.

Exercise

This chapter began with a discussion of movement, and it ends with the plea for adolescents to move, to exercise. Many adolescents do this without much prompting by getting involved in athletic and recreational activities such as dancing that require considerable movement related to the development of muscle and body tone. But adolescence can also become a very sedentary period for some (and especially for those who are overweight), and the significant adults in their lives should do whatever is necessary to encourage an exercise regime, an active life. Modeling it in your own life is the best way—for them, and for you.

Does it really make any sense to drive an adolescent a half mile to sports practice when the major focus of such activities is to move on your feet? It makes about as much sense as an adult driving a relatively short distance to a gym for exercise.

CHAPTER THREE

Sexuality and Bonding

Maintaining Our Species

S uccessful organisms must determine how to survive and get into the gene pool. The initial development of key survival skills and information dominates childhood, and these continue to mature during our second 10 years, along with the added adolescent tasks of learning how to become a productive, and reproductive, human being.

Puberty activates our reproductive system. Unfortunately, our biological ability to reproduce emerges a decade or more before most of us are psychologically and financially capable of rearing children. Our ability to bond with a partner and children also continues to develop during adolescence.

A typically concomitant adolescent vocational drive weakens parental dependency and the continuing need for the level of sheltering that parents had provided during childhood. Autonomy thus begins to evolve with a growing awareness of its civic, vocational, and perhaps parental responsibilities. Adolescents begin to look beyond the family that defined their childhood.

Survival skills are individually mastered and executed. We can't survive for someone else. Conversely, reproduction is a social act. We have to get someone to become very friendly with us to do it, and most adolescents who are intent on mating behavior have figured out that the cardinal rule is to not mate with a loser. It's thus important for adolescents on the prowl to communicate the impression that if they don't already have their act together, they're working on it.

Adolescence thus enhances the sense of personal and social identity that will define our adult life. We're a social species, and so most of us seek to share our intimate life with another and also to develop a wider circle of friends and acquaintances. Gender identity thus becomes a basic adolescent issue.

Most people are comfortable with their innate gender status and its concomitant cultural role expectations—and they seek intimacy and bonding with the opposite gender. Upwards of 10 percent aren't comfortable with that, however, and seek intimacy and bonding from within their own or both genders. People historically tended to hide their homosexual or bisexual feelings because of cultural disapproval, but that reticence has changed considerably in recent years.

Today's adolescents will thus participate in the resolution of several cultural controversies related to gender, whether they are male or female, a part of the heterosexual majority or the bisexual or homosexual minority. They will also have to determine how they will personally respond to those who differ and to the disparaging gender-related speech and behavior of others.

A generation ago, our society experienced a contentious reexamination of the concept of race and its relationship to equality in civil rights and benefits. Further, the decision to grant women the right to vote occurred in the United States only a generation before that. We are now engaged in a similarly explosive rights/benefits examination within the context of marriage—whether the civil rights and benefits that automatically accrue to heterosexual couples through marriage should be extended to psychologically bonded homosexual couples who wish to marry.

Our society is simultaneously confronting additional gender issues, such as the value of same-sex classes in school, the appropriate focus of sex education programs, the role of females and homosexuals in military service and the ministry, gender patterns in criminal behavior, gender aptitude in areas such as science and math, and the higher incidence of males or females who suffer from various body or brain disorders. The emerging influence of fundamentalist theologies raises additional issues about the appropriate roles of men and women in society.

All these issues incorporate complex biological, theological, cultural, and political elements. Unfortunately, the discourse is currently confounded by the increased and widespread availability of electronically disseminated opinions that don't necessarily provide credible supporting data. Today's adolescents thus enter into a cultural discourse that's more often characterized by cacophony than cogency. They can vote at 18 on issues such as those identified above, and citizens in a democracy don't have to be informed to vote.

In our social species and within many adolescent minds, sexual behavior and bonding may well be the central issues around which almost everything else revolves. The extended discussion that follows should thus provide useful information that you can incorporate into discussions with adolescents who are trying to find their way through this very complex and volatile set of issues.

Gender has historically been defined as the separation of humans into male and female groups, with consequent cultural roles and behavioral expectations. Traditional gender perceptions and issues are now compounded by research technologies that can compare male and female body/brain structures and cognitive activity in ways not previously possible, and by rare, culturally confusing, and controversial conditions such as transsexuality and intersexuality. (Some children are born with an ambiguous sexual system that often creates issues related to gender identity and sexual orientation as they mature.)

The traditional conventional wisdom—that we consciously choose our sexual orientation—has eroded as people have thought more about their own personal experiences and about other biological predispositions, such as handedness and temperament, which they similarly didn't consciously choose. The roles that culture and genetics play in gender behavior have similarly become problematic as parents observe developmental variations in children's play patterns and adolescent friendship preferences.

It thus appears that most individuals are clearly either male or female but that some exist (for whatever biological and/or cultural reasons) within an androgynous category that's biologically and behaviorally separate from the two pure gender strains. Gender thus isn't the simple, straightforward, conscious phenomenon that most folks formerly believed and that some folks continue to believe. Variability is ubiquitous within biological species, and gender is simply one manifestation of it.

Some cultural gender differences seem to have little to do with biology, such as the constantly shifting clothing and hairstyles, the division of household tasks, and the recent gender shifts in some vocations—such as that more women are becoming medical doctors and attorneys, and more men are becoming nurses and early childhood teachers.

BIOLOGICAL DIFFERENCES

Other differences are biological. It's obvious that different reproductive roles require related differences in male and female bodies and brains. For example, although the **hormones testosterone, estrogen, oxytocin**, and **vasopressin** are present in everyone, women typically have more estrogen and oxytocin, and men have more testosterone and vasopressin. Further, women have a monthly menstrual cycle, and men have both daily and yearly testosterone cycles (high, morning and autumn; low, evening and spring). The more complex question is whether other significant normative brain differences exist that aren't as easily related to reproductive roles.

The average male brain is slightly larger than the average female brain, but overall size may be less significant than internal organizational differences. For example, the **corpus callosum**, which connects the two hemispheres, is slightly larger in women, and the hypothalamic structure that seems to regulate sexual orientation is larger in men than in women. Women tend to have a more dominant left hemisphere; men, a more dominant right hemisphere. The auditory and olfactory systems tend to be more robust in women, and the visual movement detection system tends to be more robust in men.

Further, our survival depends on our ability to understand how objects and systems function (systematizing capability) and to infer other people's thoughts and intentions (empathizing capability). Although almost all men and women can do both adequately, men seem to have a slight edge in systematizing and women in empathizing.

Memory involves recalling the general concept and also the factual information that underlies the concept. Women seem to have an edge in factual recall and men in conceptual recall. Navigation strategies use geometric cues and the recall of landmarks. Men seem to depend more on geometric cues, and women more on landmarks. The typical male stress response is a fight-or-flight, assertive response, but in females, it's often a tend-or-befriend, nurturing response. The significance of these and other biological differences is problematic and controversial.

Interpreting Gender Differences

These and other reported overlapping gender differences create interpretive dilemmas. What we do know is that:

1. Men and women are structurally and behaviorally much more similar than they are different.

2. Differences that do exist don't imply that one cognitive property or strategy is necessarily better than another.

3. Measurable differences must be interpreted in light of the *within/between factor* in normative research studies that compare group scores on human properties, capabilities, and behaviors, such as those listed above.

Figure 3.1 shows that the range of scores *within* each of the two groups is larger than the difference *between* the mean scores of the two groups. For example, consider height differences in large, normally distributed male and female groups. The difference between the tallest and shortest person in each gender group will be greater than the difference between the average heights of the two groups of males and females. Thus, some women will be taller than some men in normative groups, even though the total population of men averages 7 percent taller than women.

Figure 3.1   Within/Between Factor in Normative Group Scores

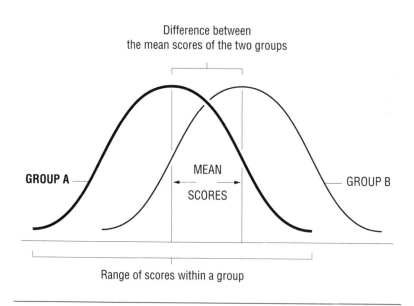

Difference between
the mean scores of the two groups

GROUP A

MEAN

SCORES

GROUP B

Range of scores within a group

Group differences thus show only group tendencies; they don't predict for any single person in either group. So although it's possible and appropriate to report general observations about normative male/female differences, it's inappropriate to stereotype—to use a general observation about a group to predict the properties, capabilities, and behavior of any individual man or woman within the group. Further, it's inappropriate to argue that only innate or only cultural factors (and not a mix of the two) led to the difference.

Key survival and reproductive tasks are regulated by a variety of interconnected conscious and subconscious brain systems. Chapter 2 suggested that we must be able to successfully recognize and respond to both novel and familiar dangers and opportunities that confront us within our space/time environment. We individually confront such dichotomous challenges, but different normative group capabilities can emerge over many generations—such as in populations who inhabit arctic and desert environments, and in gender groups whose cultural roles differ significantly.

CULTURAL CONFUSION

Gender-related cultural phenomena such as marriage, sports teams, and clothing styles are currently in flux. Two generations ago, we went through a contentious period in which many people were disturbed when men started to wear longer hair; and we're now going through a period in which some female students want to join the wrestling team or become the football team's place-kicker. Same-sex bonding and marriage are perhaps just another step on a path of gender redefinition that we've already been traveling for some time. Is marriage thus a phenomenon that should involve only two separate and pure gender categories, or should marriage be redefined as a personal public bonding commitment between two consenting adults, irrespective of the gender category each occupies?

So the issue comes down to how we should now define the concepts of male and female for the emerging generation, considering that recent biological thought and discovery on the issue suggests that a fuzzy line both separates and unites the concepts of male and female, and especially as they relate to bonding behaviors. Since bonding is a major adolescent preoccupation, the current cultural controversy is significant to them, even though they may be several years from having to deal with it in their own lives or in the lives of family or friends.

Human Bonding Behavior

Human reproduction requires separate male and female sexual systems, but also a mutual willingness to engage in sexual behavior, and an understanding that strong cultural pressures exist to bond legally if pregnancy results. Since child rearing involves an extended parental commitment, the impetus to engage in sexual behavior must be innate and strong. Call it love—an intense, joyful attraction between two people that's typically associated with romantic and familial bonding.

We've long associated love with our heart, but it really encompasses our entire body and brain, our entire psychological being, our entire life span—and researchers are now unlocking many of its intriguing mysteries. Romantic love appears to follow a three-stage *lust-attraction-attachment* sequence that emerged out of our strong biological drive to reproduce and our need to nurture children throughout their extended developmental period (Fisher, 2004). Bonded couples who have no plans to conceive children (such as older or same-sex couples) apparently also follow the same biological/psychological sequence.

Scientists can now use brain-imaging technology to identify the specific brain and chemical systems that drive the complete process. The **hypothalamus, caudate nucleus, nucleus accumbens, septum,** and several frontal lobe areas are especially active when love is on our mind—and **dopamine, norepinephrine, serotonin, endorphins,** oxytocin, vasopressin, testosterone, and estrogen are the molecules that seemingly jump for joy as they excite and inhibit the body/brain systems that regulate the behavior of love. So it's party time all over our body and brain when love is in the air.

Lust is a somewhat abstract process that initially emerges during early adolescence, when the appearance of secondary sexual characteristics sparks sexual curiosity. Testosterone and estrogen provide an encouraging push to just go looking. **Pheromones** and personality predispositions probably assist in narrowing the field (such as by eliminating close relatives). Further, innate variations in the systems and molecules that regulate sexual behavior may bias a person's focus to a same-sex rather than to an opposite-sex partner. Sometimes sky-rockets go off immediately, and sometimes things heat up slowly—but at some point, generalized biological lust leads to focused psychological attraction.

Attraction is highly focused attention. One's beloved becomes foreground and absolutely everything else becomes background. This is a time for fine-tuning initial impressions, and so the couple spends many hours checking out each other. If the attraction remains mutually supportive long enough to resolve any nagging concerns, the third stage, attachment, kicks in.

Attachment is for the long haul, since it must maintain the relationship though inevitable distractions. Oxytocin, vaso-pressin, and endorphins become part of the bonding glue that maintains the relationship whenever temporary troubles arise. Wedding promises before family and friends, joint own-ership of possessions, and children in need of parental love and nurture often provide a needed cultural bandage while a marriage hurt heals.

Children typically enter into a loving relationship with both parents at the attraction stage—the soulful gazing into a parental face, the oxytocin boost from nursing, the cuddling behavior that elevates oxytocin, vasopressin, and endorphin levels in both parents and child. Human survival depends on children bonding with their parents and their parents bonding with them. The possibility of same-sex bonding thus emerges in infancy—father/son, mother/daughter, plus favorite same-sex relatives.

Innate forces and shared family activities typically create a situation in which they typically can hardly resist each other—until puberty, when lust kicks in and adolescents have to go looking elsewhere to help continue the biological des-tiny of their species.

A dilemma for both adolescents and their parents is that adolescents need to weaken their parental bonds in order to bond and then fall in love with someone else. This can create an adolescent bonding void that makes them vulnerable to impetuous, troublesome alliances with peers or with older and/or predatory partners.

Further, media depictions of gender roles and sexuality often provide adolescents with an unrealistic perspective of adult life—and the relatively easy availability of pornographic depictions exacerbates such fantasy. Helpful parental modeling of adult life can be absent in a complex society in which children have no clear understanding of their parents' vocational—and even personal—life. Divorce similarly creates serious parental modeling problems. Grandparents and others in the extended family may live hundreds of miles away—getting together only during ceremonial occasions.

For many adolescents, secondary school teachers, coaches, and youth workers become useful primary or secondary adult models. An adolescent may spend several hours a day interacting with a nonparental adult, compared to minutes with parents.

Vulnerable early adolescents thus benefit from institutionalized arrangements in which they interact within several organized groups rather than only in pairs. Club and class activities, parties, dances, group excursions, and school extracurricular programs are examples of pleasant opportunities for adolescents to observe a variety of peers in different settings. Many adolescents get jobs in the service industry at 16 or so, and these similarly provide useful opportunities for them to observe other adolescents and nonkin adults in a work setting. The commitment in all such adolescent activity is principally to the organization or event, and not to any participating individual.

The flip side of bonding involves such negative behaviors as ridicule, stereotyping, and bullying. Adolescents who are unsure of themselves may engage in such behaviors as attention-getting techniques. Youth organizations can play an important role in reducing such behavior through their ability to require appropriate behavior from participants. Adolescents typically don't want to be dismissed from a group, and so they tend to follow the rules—and so learn how to make and keep friends.

EMERGING CULTURAL CONFLICTS

Love and its developmental trajectory are complex, and they encompass many issues of appropriateness and legality that currently confront our culture. Some folks think that reducing love to neurochemicals and activated brain systems demeans the concept of love, but I think not. How wonderful to realize that falling and staying in love involves a perhaps forever-mystical synchronization of two complete biological organisms—and that's what the poets and songwriters have basically told us all along.

The biochemical complexities of love allow people who are infertile or homosexual to still fall in love and yearn to rear children, and people who have lost a partner through death or divorce to fall in love again. People are willing to teach, nurse, and coach the children of others. Two people who have few friends and seemingly no bonding prospects will suddenly discover each other. Love is such a marvelously supportive and adaptable human property!

Since it's in our society's interest to encourage the stability of commitment, married couples now automatically gain more than a thousand civil rights and benefits. Committed same-sex couples have recently been asking why they are currently denied the civil rights and benefits that accrue to married couples, given that their level of commitment to each other and their parental responsibilities might be equal to or even surpass those of many married couples.

Those opposed to extending marriage to same-sex couples typically do so on historical and religious grounds—arguing that marriage has historically been viewed as a male/female religious concept, and ought to remain so, and that some religious organizations have strong sanctions against homosexuality and same-sex unions.

Same-sex marriage advocates counter with the argument that couples must go to the courthouse for a civil license before going to a church building for the marriage ceremony, and that couples can legally marry in a ceremony totally devoid of religious ritual. They further contend that a secular democracy should not grant civil rights and benefits to one class of citizens that it denies to another on the basis of religious beliefs. Some therefore suggest that the license should validate a civil union and that marriage be considered a religious option.

Those opposed argue that changing the definition of marriage could create a whole series of cultural and legal dilemmas. For example, how should our society respond if more than two people, or if siblings, or if an adult and child want to marry?

Some argue that the issue should focus on the emerging awareness of the innate biology of sexuality, and others argue that biology is irrelevant—people ought to have a right to bond with whomever they choose. And truth be told, we all know couples of whom we think: "What can they possibly see in each other?"—but they obviously see something beautiful.

And that's where this issue currently stands—contentiously complex and messy, with its final resolution probably far down the road. The resolutions of related school, military, and institutional gender issues are similarly complex and probably distant. But the reality is that today's adolescents will participate in the resolutions of these issues, and so they need to begin the process of contemplating the complexities.

In the meantime, they're looking for credible information and adult direction. Adults who work with adolescents can expect criticism, no matter what they do or don't do to explain the complexities of gender issues and sexual behavior. Let's work to ensure that the emerging societal discussion will proceed in a civil manner appropriate to a democratic society—devoid of name-calling and hatred, with empathy for all who are affected by the issues—which means all of us.

THE HAZARDS OF SEXUAL PLEASURE

Our sexual response systems are tuned to pleasurable stimuli. An infant who enjoys the parental closeness associated with breast-feeding, cuddling, caressing, and hugging will grow up to enjoy the same kinds of intimate behavior with an adolescent friend.

Extended sexual intimacy often leads to the oral/genital exchange of body fluids, an exchange that can lead to conception and/or to sexually transmitted diseases. Such intimacies should thus ideally be limited to those who are sufficiently mature to accept the potential results and responsibilities.

Would that things were that simple. As indicated earlier, our sexual drive emerges in adolescence, well before the emergence of adult rational judgment and personal responsibility. Parents are especially concerned about this mismatch because they realize how much their child's sexual mishaps will complicate the lives of all involved—and because they recall their own adolescent sexual drives and experiences. What was pleasant to them then becomes scary now. They're disquieted by current reports that 20 percent of adolescents have had intercourse by age 15 and well over half have engaged in oral sexual behavior.

The cultural strategies for reducing the undesirable effects of sexual intercourse are to promote abstinence, to provide protection, and to educate young people about sexuality.

Abstinence

Most parents and religious organizations prefer that adolescents be abstinent, even though many such parents weren't abstinent during their own adolescence. Efforts to promote abstinence tend to focus on morality—that it's wrong to engage in sexual behavior that can negatively affect the life of another. Many adolescents today take vows of chastity, typically through the efforts of a religious organization. Unfortunately, such rational decisions in a public setting may disintegrate within the private emotional intimacies of a couple's relationship. It's not that an abstinence decision doesn't work, because it has and does for many virginal adolescents. The problem is the vulnerability of such a decision in an immature adolescent.

Protection

Although most parents prefer that their adolescents remain virginal, many also seek the backup strategy that effective contraception provides. Contraceptive devices such as condoms and diaphragms stop or at least reduce body fluid transfer, and contraceptive pills have chemical properties that prevent ovulation.

As effective as contraceptives typically are if used correctly, none is 100 percent effective—and diaphragms and pills don't protect against sexually transmitted diseases. The exact mechanisms of emergency forms of postintercourse contraception (typically called morning-after pills) are still poorly understood, but they can prevent pregnancy if taken within 72 hours after intercourse (but preferably as soon as possible).

The possibilities of abortion, adoption, and single parenthood extend the initial problem of an adolescent pregnancy and create an even more complex set of issues. Our society is and will probably always be divided over the appropriate resolution of these issues. For example, what roles should the parents of the adolescents, the child's father, and the government play in the resolution of an adolescent pregnancy?

One problem with the adolescent use of contraceptives is that adolescent intercourse is often opportunistic, and emotion often trumps judgment in adolescents. Further, it may be embarrassing to get together with a partner already prepared with pills or condoms. Adolescents may thus engage in mutual masturbation and oral or anal sexual activity because they eliminate the fear of pregnancy—albeit certainly not the fear of a sexually transmitted disease. And then things escalate.

Education

Adolescent sex education programs have historically attempted to provide explicit information on sexual drive, reproductive systems, contraception, and the hazards of sexual behavior. Critics suggest that providing adolescents with such information implicitly validates extramarital sexuality in adolescents. They argue rather for a program that promotes the morality of abstinence, and the current political climate supports this perspective.

The dilemma is that adolescents will seek out explicit information on their sexuality, whether we like it or not. Our society thus must decide whether such information should come from within a carefully designed and taught secondary school curriculum or from some combination of typically reticent parents, frequently clueless peers, print and electronic mass media, pornography, and adolescent exploration.

For what it's worth, my belief—after a long personal life and professional career—is that sexuality during the adolescent years is too important to be left to chance information and direction. An unwanted adolescent pregnancy outside of marriage produces a baby who begins life at a serious disadvantage, and so the adult community ought to do whatever we can to reduce such pregnancies. Adolescents should thus be provided with a complete explanation of all aspects of sexuality, and preferably in school. Health education and biology curricula have been able to separate the biology from the morality of other body systems and processes (such as nutrition or drug effects programs), and they should also be encouraged to do it in sex education curricula—to teach rather than to preach. I also believe that adolescent abstinence should be encouraged at all levels, but that contraceptives should be readily available for adolescents who don't remain abstinent. Prohibiting protection makes as much sense to me as prohibiting drug rehabilitation programs to adolescents who still became addicted after we had provided them with useful information on the dangers of drug use.

Sexuality, in all its glorious complexity, is simultaneously one of the great joys and problems of human existence. Soar with its joys. Live with its problems.

CHAPTER FOUR

Productivity and Vocation

Maintaining Our Planet

Our upright stance and consequent necessarily narrow female birth canal have led to a one-pound birth brain that is only one third its adult size. Most animals are born with an almost fully developed brain and can thus survive immediately or at weaning. Human mothers, contemplating the size of their birth canal, have universally lauded the notion of a small birth brain.

Many human brain systems function initially at only a survival level, but then mature by expanding—connecting and insulating related neurons as environmental challenges dictate—and this explains the postbirth increase in brain size. Infants can thus innately suckle and cry, but they must later learn how to use their mouths and voices to sing songs. Fear and its startle reflex are innate, but children must be taught how best to cross a busy intersection. Our mirror neuron system and available adult models are thus central to the maturation of many capabilities.

We need a long, sheltered childhood and explicit instruction to expand the effectiveness of our neural systems so that they can function at the sophisticated level our complex culture requires. This requires the kind of extended bonding between parents, and between parents and child, that Chapter 3 discussed. Add kinship extensions, and children grow up in an interdependent society. Someone will care for them during their first two decades, but then the social contract is that they will spend the next several decades caring for their children (and for the children of others in our complex, taxed society).

So we are of necessity a social species. This innate sense of dependence means that everyone in a social group must be able to do some communal things (such as being able to speak the common language), but not everyone has to be able to do everything (such as being able to build a house). Building a house requires specialized knowledge and skills that require extensive training, but we don't often need to build a house. Thus, it's to everyone's advantage for a few people to specialize in construction skills, and to maintain their abilities by doing it as a vocation, and for others to specialize in something else. It's a complex, tit-for-tat negotiating arrangement—you build my house, and I'll build your kitchen appliances. This shift from dependence to productive interdependence typically begins during adolescence.

At some point, the adolescent reach for autonomy confronts the realization that autonomy comes at a cost. Those who want to make their own decisions must fund the costs of the decision. Parental largesse has its limits. Chapter 1 reported my midadolescent realization of this vocational reality, and I expect that you have a similar story to tell.

In a simple society, adults use an apprenticeship model to prepare adolescents for such adult challenges. Apprentices observe and assist their elders at work and gradually assume greater responsibility as their skills and judgment improve. Eventually the apprentice runs the enterprise, and the mentor plays the supportive role. It's an effective means of blending the generational waxing and waning of vocational skills in concert with adolescent frontal lobe maturation. A central value of this model is that the apprentice becomes intimately aware of all the production stages and informally observes the mentor's acquired skill and wisdom in the process.

In our current complex society, many living necessities are produced beyond the immediate neighborhood. Understanding shipping and shopping rather than farming and fabricating thus become central, and much human interaction is indirect and distant. Many—and especially the young—have no direct awareness of production components and stages. Objects arrive assembled and packaged. The apprentice of yore sharpened the knife so the master could cut or carve—but the processed meat in today's snack pack is presliced (and the nature and origin of the incomprehensible ingredients are often a mystery). Further, many of today's adolescents would be hard-pressed to describe the specific occupational meaning and activity of the significant adults in their life.

"Take Your Child to Work" days provide young people with some sense of parental vocation, but it's important for parents to explicitly communicate the vocational roles they play in the community and family enterprise (and being a homemaker is an important family and community vocation). Adolescents may or may not follow their parents' vocational life, but they should understand what it involves and what its advantages and disadvantages are.

Many adolescents get jobs, but these tend to be simple service jobs at the end of a production sequence that have little relationship to what they'll probably do in their adult vocational lives—except perhaps for learning to show up on time and to follow customer and managerial directives.

The informal apprenticeship became a less appropriate educational model for an increasingly widespread and complex society. The formal school that thus emerged in our society focuses more on the skills and knowledge necessary for social interaction than on practical production skills. Indeed, curricula (such as the arts) that actually produce something become vulnerable, and assessment typically focuses more on knowing the correct response to a question that the school posed than on the cognitive processes the student used to develop the response—or on the student's ability to identify significant problems.

Cultural and educational models will work only if our brain can comprehend them and/or can create technologies that extend comprehension and performance beyond our biological limitations. For example, when it became culturally advantageous to produce materials in one location for use elsewhere, the efficient movement of such materials and information became essential. The development of transportation technologies and a three-R's curriculum thus made sense in an era in which folks had to learn how to precisely communicate needs and compute quantities to those who lived elsewhere. Further, students had to know all about the geography and sociology of *elsewhere* if they were going to interact with it.

A 21st-Century Curriculum
for 21st-Century Students

The key elements of that traditional curriculum are still germane to a 21st-century curriculum, but 21st-century students will live their adult lives and careers within a much more complex culture, which will make demands that were uncommon during the 20th century. It's thus important that adolescent curricula now focus more on the development of intuitive, logical, and predictive capabilities that will enhance the resolution of emerging complex cultural issues. Consider the curricular and parental implications of the following emerging vocational challenges:

• Students are already confronting the issue of how to assess the credibility of electronic resources. Print information is cumbersome, slow, and expensive—and so it must exhibit credibility to those who will purchase and use it. Conversely, electronic information is simpler, faster, and cheaper—and so it's much easier to develop and distribute. The consumer has thus had to assume an increasing responsibility for determining the credibility of electronically distributed information. Further, students who are developing curricular projects now depend much more on the Internet than on print resources. Can you even imagine their going to the library to check out something in the print version of a resource that's also available online?

- Twentieth-century schools ensured the credibility of the print materials they used. We now live in an Orwellian era replete with electronic predators of all stripes, who easily and cynically distribute misleading information. In the 21st century, schools must teach students how to ascertain the credibility of the electronic information they use in their course work and life (and so also eventually in their vocation). This involves teaching them how to assess the credibility of the author, how to seek out and compare conflicting perspectives, and how to determine the validity and reliability of statistical information. The current adult generation didn't get this kind of instruction, because it wasn't deemed as critical in a print-oriented society. The result is that current deceptive marketing and political campaigns hoodwink many adults.

- The 20th century began with Albert Einstein's revolutionary perspectives in physics, and the physical sciences dominated 20th-century thought and activity. The focus was on the manufacture of objects and machines and on the transportation systems that moved them from here to there. I had no childhood or adolescent contact with my dozens of cousins who lived a couple of thousand miles away, because I was already an adult when the U.S. Interstate highway system emerged at midcentury. People previously lived near where they worked, and even recreational travel was limited by the quality and availability of automobiles and roads.

We enter a much different 21st century, initially dominated by recent dramatic developments in the electronic technologies and biological sciences. Extended travel is increasingly common among young people, and their daily Internet communication is global. Even the video games they play with friends on the Internet highway don't require them to be together in the same room, or even in the same community. Global issues have become local issues, and vice versa. An increasing number of vocations require an understanding of the global implications of products and services.

- The discovery of DNA led to a biological explosion. Computer technology—combined with a clearer understanding of biological systems—led to the development of amazing research technologies that could describe the human **genome** embedded within every cell's nucleus and observe cognitive processes that were formerly hidden within a bony skull. The initial applications of this biotechnology emerged in medicine, but they're rapidly moving into all segments of 21st-century life—and they're sparking an increasing number of biologically based cultural issues and vocations related to cloning, stem cells, medications, education, and lifespan.

• The physical sciences have also exploded culturally and vocationally, via the new computerized technologies. We've gone in a few years from a dramatic initial moonwalk to telescopic explorations farther into space than we could have even imagined at the beginning of the 20th century. We've gone from a 20th-century assembly line operated by humans to a 21st-century assembly line operated by robots. The big-box TV sets of a couple decades ago have been miniaturized into credit card–size music and video players—and into cell phones that can do all sorts of things. *Pac-Man* and *Donkey Kong* are certainly amazed at what they've morphed into in just a few years.

• Perhaps most important, it's difficult to predict what new kinds of vocations will emerge in the coming years. You can easily identify vocations that didn't exist when you began your adolescence. This suggests that we should probably help adolescents to think vocationally in *verb* behaviors that are broader than *noun* labels. Accountant, banker, chef, doctor, engineer, and on to zoologist are vocational labels. Better to help adolescents to think instead about what they like to *do* and can *do* well. I discovered through adolescent organizations that I enjoyed social challenges and that I liked to explain things. It was a hop and a skip into teaching. A less socially oriented adolescent friend who was fascinated with model airplanes became an aircraft designer. The (noun) vocational titles may change over a career, but the basic (verb) vocational activity is more of a constant. Adolescent life and education should thus be a time of self-discovery, best achieved in a rich environmental mix of social and individual exploration. The breadth of the liberal arts provides many such curricular opportunities.

A 21ST-CENTURY VOCATION

The emergence of strong labor unions during the 20th century led to job security and a decent income for many people who spent their careers working for a single company. They enjoyed health and vacation benefits and retired on a decent pension. Companies often hired the children of employees, and so large businesses located in towns and cities were essential to the community's continued success. Locally owned support services and businesses enhanced the sense of community and circulated their earnings locally.

The 21st century began with the increased outsourcing of production and support service jobs to countries that don't provide the pay, benefits, or job security that labor unions worked so hard to secure. Many small towns have been economically devastated by the loss of the principal employer and the closure of locally owned stores and restaurants that couldn't compete with the national chains, which lowered prices through mass purchase and other efficiencies—and then siphoned local profits into distant corporate coffers.

The possibility of such a career in a hometown firm, or eventually owning a local business, has thus become a more problematic dream for adolescents who want to stay in the area. Well, it may be difficult, but it's not impossible for those who think creatively (and in *verb* terms).

The good news for such adolescents is that outsourcing and the spread of national and international corporations across the country aren't the only reasons for the economic shifts that have occurred in many communities. For example, Eugene, Oregon, was principally a timber town when we moved here 38 years ago. Its economy has become far less dependent on the production of lumber products over the years because of the reduced availability of timber, increased regulations, foreign competition, and market changes. Rather than wither, the area has creatively adapted into something that's now economically quite different and more diverse than what it used to be.

For example, it turns out that an environment suitable for conifers now also grows most of the world's grass seed, produces highly rated Pinot wines, and produces a large variety of harvested wild mushrooms, among other things. The lumber mills that produced houses have morphed into companies that produce high-end motor homes. The timber industry is still important, but not as dominant as it was—and it too has changed. Necessity and creativity have encouraged the lumber industry to turn formerly burned or abandoned forest by-products and timber scraps into particleboard and other wood products. Christmas tree farms abound. Environmental concerns and policies have maintained the natural beauty of the area, and this has enhanced the growth of tourism and its economic impact. Other important changes have occurred as well, but I'm sure that you get the point. The *nouns* changed; the *verbs* remained constant. What happened here has parallels across the country. Communities creatively adapt to challenge or die.

Today's adolescents must similarly adapt their vocational goals to current realities, regardless of where they want to live. The rapid cultural changes of recent years make it easy for them to do this. Five hundred years ago, European adolescents dreamed about getting on a boat and sailing west. Today's adolescents dream about electronically traversing the globe in milliseconds, checking out what's beyond our universe, and exploring the inner world of molecular biology. But they are also fascinated by new possibilities within the arts and social systems that the new technologies pose. And within all the glitz of the current scientific and technological explosion, many adolescents still seek careers at the human scale of social and educational services.

On a related personal note: If I were once again an adolescent thinking about my career possibilities, a career in education would still appeal to me, but for a different reason. What a challenge to be able to participate in the most explosive changes the education profession will have ever experienced! During my career, we've gone from a folklore profession to one that has a reasonably good understanding of what we're doing. I can't even imagine what will occur during the careers of the next generation of educators. How exciting to be a participant rather than only an observer.

What's true of my profession is also true of most other vocations. It's a somewhat scary period for adolescents, because everything seems in flux. But isn't that kind of uncertainty exactly what adolescents also seek when they surf, ski, and skateboard?

I'm fascinated by the recent emergence of adolescent blogs. Adolescents are informally exploring new forms of communication through their blogs, and they'll similarly explore the interactive electronic technologies still on the horizon. Whether or not they realize it, they're simultaneously learning how to organize and operate communication systems within the electronic environment they'll inhabit. All sorts of inventions and careers will emerge out of these explorations.

The practical applications of such pure exploration aren't always immediately apparent. Apple Computer cofounder Steven Jobs learned a lot about typography during a course in calligraphy he once took on a whim. When he helped design the Macintosh Computer 10 years later, his earlier explorations with calligraphy led to the first computer with aesthetic type fonts.

Our generations left home to work, but many people today work at or out of their homes and interact electronically with colleagues and clients. Further, it will be unusual if they spend their entire career in one job. Such vocational shifts require an entrepreneurial, self-disciplined mentality that differs from what occurs in a business environment in which managers directly supervise workers.

The frontal lobes that mature during adolescence reach for the kind of creative autonomy that the emerging economic environment needs. One might thus think that this is the worst of times for an adolescent to move toward an adult vocation, given all the current cultural and economic shifts. But one might also optimistically think that this is the best of times for creative, independent adolescents who want to help shape the adult world they'll inhabit. Such adolescents don't want stability if it means a job in which they'll do only what others tell them to do. That dependence reminds them too much of the home and school they're leaving. Their frontal lobes are reaching for personal and vocational autonomy, for challenge rather than security.

Subsequent chapters, which explore specific areas of adolescent maturation, will discuss the vocational implications of those areas.

HOME, SCHOOL, AND VOCATION

Chapter 2 described the mirror neuron system that activates during the execution of goal-directed movements and also during the observation of such movements in others. It's the neurobiological substrate of mimicking, and it's central to the development and smooth regulation of motor behaviors. Early childhood learning is thus quite dependent on the motor behavior that children observe in their parents and others.

Children and adolescents also carefully observe how their parents interact with each other, with other people, and with their vocations. Most adults would agree that such continual parental observations positively or negatively influenced their own beliefs and behavior.

Parents who hope that their adolescents will mature into productive adults can enhance the process by demonstrating a positive collaborative perspective of their own personal, vocational, and civic lives. I use the term *lives*, because vocation involves more than one area of life. Parents must maintain their home, directly or indirectly work in a vocation that supports their family, and participate in (typically volunteer) activities that support elements of the larger community.

Children and adolescents should also participate in all three throughout their maturation. Maintaining a home requires a lot of cleaning, repairing, moving, cooking, and other tasks.

Your children's adult partners will thank you for instilling a sense of genuine family participation in such activities—and especially if all such activities are viewed as gender free. It should be a taken-for-granted part of family membership. We've all known (and don't appreciate) people who expect others to pick up after them. If children observe their parents working effectively as a team to maintain the home, they'll be more apt to join in. They'll grouse about it, but we adults also often grouse about doing household chores.

It's more difficult today for children to get the kinds of jobs (such as delivering newspapers) that they could obtain years ago. I made spending money at age 10 by walking around the neighborhood looking for lawns that needed mowing. I soon had regular customers who also hired me to do other chores. The sidewalk lemonade stands of children that morph into adolescent eBay sales may not make a lot of money, but they help to instill an entrepreneurial spirit. Walking with children and grandchildren to a recent university football game, I saw an early adolescent violinist standing next to the walkway playing the university's sports song. A protective parent stood unobtrusively off to one side. Folks smiled and put money in her violin case. She discovered that afternoon that she could elicit smiles while practicing the violin and earn some money at the same time. Can't beat that.

Being a responsible adult includes a willingness to contribute to community needs. We do some of this through taxes that spread the costs of benefits we all enjoy, but most adults also contribute money and volunteer their time and energy in other ways. Parents coach sports teams, help their neighbors, volunteer at schools, and engage in many similar community activities. It's good for young people to see their parents so involved—and it's even better when children collaborate with their parents in such volunteer work.

So we begin our lives by mimicking parental smiles and arm movements—and by adolescence we should also be mimicking the positive perspectives and behavior of our parents as they maintain a home, engage in a vocation, and assist in community tasks.

CHAPTER FIVE

Morality and Ethics

Maintaining Our Culture

W hen a challenge confronts us, we must determine both the best possible response and our ability to carry it out successfully. Since we're a social and moral species, we should also consider how our response would affect other organisms.

Knowing how to do something—and deciding whether or not to do it—are thus separate but related issues, and they're central to understanding and responding to the true/false and right/wrong dichotomies that play such important roles in our lives. Such factually oriented fields as science and math attempt to identify the precise point that separates the true/false dichotomy, and such belief-oriented fields as philosophy and theology attempt to identify the ambiguous point that separates the right/wrong dichotomy that's central to morality and ethics. Aesthetic dichotomies (such as beautiful/ugly) also exist, and Chapter 8 will explore those.

Morality as a concept is concerned with the general definitional principles of right/wrong, good/bad, fair/unfair, and so on, and *ethics*, with the development of specific behavioral codes that folks should follow. For example, since it's immoral to kill someone, the medical profession has developed ethical guidelines that reduce the possibility of death from medical mistakes and malpractice.

Our sheltered childhood focuses primarily on the development of the cognitive systems (principally in the sensory lobe) that recognize and interpret objective factual information. The adolescent reach for autonomy matures the cognitive systems (principally in the frontal lobe) that process the subjective beliefs that lead to preferences and choices. It makes sense for a brain to understand the factual information that underlies an ambiguous challenge before trying to solve it.

FACTUAL KNOWLEDGE AND DECISIONS

Factual, or veridical, knowledge is knowing the answer to a problem that has a single correct answer, for example: $6 \times 5 = 30$, Salem is the capital of Oregon, c-a-t spells cat. It's the product-oriented essence of true/false—and it's the quintessential element of such culturally popular activities as crossword puzzles and TV quiz shows (in which the winning contestant has the best command of the least important, most obscure factual information). Students typically spend a lot of school time discovering and remembering the hidden answers to clear-cut factual questions they didn't ask—and for which they often have no personal context.

Factual knowledge is an obviously important cognitive element of problem solving and moral/ethical behavior, but true/false isn't always as clear-cut as many folks think. For example, mastering one's native language is a major juvenile task. The hundreds of thousands of words in our language are factual, in that each represents a clearly defined category. Still, it's much easier to precisely define some concepts (such as *male*) than others (such as *chair*). But even a precisely defined concept (*male*) may have many synonyms (such as man, gentleman, guy, chap, and fellow) that are used interchangeably in common discourse, even though each synonym has a distinct meaning.

Further, English spelling allows for few acceptable variants, but most people could easily read the word *accommodate* when misspelled in several different ways. E-mail has further confounded standard spelling with a growing number of abbreviations (such as *U* for *you*, and *gr8* for *great*) that folks easily master and readily use to speed up electronic discourse. Mark Twain's comment that only an uncreative person can think of but one way to spell a word seems apropos.

Fortunately, our brain is sufficiently adaptable that it can function with information that's only fairly close to precise truth—so, for example, we often estimate quantities rather than make the effort to get a precise count. Further, we tend to offload information that requires memorized precision to such technologies as calculators, telephone books, spell-checkers, and dictionaries. And even then, the technological precision that e-mail addresses require frustrates our imprecise brain whenever a message gets rejected because of a single-letter error in the address.

Much of our childhood is devoted to mastering language, computation, and culturally important factual information. The sensory lobes, which develop during childhood, are a principal processing center for such information. Survival often requires an accurate and rapid analysis of the current challenge. By the time they reach adolescence, most children will have developed the requisite observational and perceptual skills and a functional memory bank that can connect current challenges with past experiences. They typically can also adequately communicate their thoughts at an almost automatic level. The state standards and assessments programs for elementary school students tend to focus on their mastery of such factual knowledge and skills.

What children can't do as effectively is determine how best to respond to the ambiguous challenges that confront them. That ability requires mature frontal lobes, which develop during adolescence. Chapter 2 indicated that adults serve as de facto frontal lobes for children. Parents and other adults make most of the important decisions in their lives, and they supervise any decisions children do make. If children must make a decision when no adult is present, they'll typically do what they believe an adult would do in that situation—and they generally know what that is because they constantly observe adults making decisions. Further, we teach them what to do when they confront challenges alone, such as how to cross a street and how to phone for help.

Factual knowledge is thus important, but its cultural precision is overrated, and it's not the driving cognitive force behind autonomous adult behavior that's intelligent and wise, moral and ethical.

ADAPTIVE PREFERENCES AND CHOICES

Thought processes that lead to a preference and then to a choice among alternatives are personal, adaptive to one's circumstances. A choice isn't necessarily based on objective criteria. Knowing the names of the student council candidates is factual knowledge. Casting my vote for one is an adaptive choice. Most human thought and decision making are adaptive, actor centered. How do I interpret the facts? What choice is best for me?

We often use factual information during the process of making an adaptive decision. For example, we look at a restaurant menu before ordering and note such factual elements as the cost and composition of items. Cost may be important to the price-conscious and ingredients to the allergic—but the issue of what we should order has no correct or incorrect answer. It's a personal preference based on many factors, and almost any order is a legitimate decision. The situation is similar with the many product choices we confront in stores.

Even U.S. Supreme Court decisions are adaptive. After examining the facts of the case and the relevant, carefully worded laws and precedents, the judges may differ 5–4 on which position in the case is constitutionally correct.

It's not unusual for people to make decisions that are contrary to their factual knowledge of the situation. For example, even though all adolescents know that tobacco use can lead to serious medical problems, many still become consciously addicted. Further, prisons are full of people who deeply regret a decision they once made, fully aware at the time that it was illegal, immoral, and/or unethical.

Much of our success in life depends on our ability to make good decisions. People don't normally lose their jobs because they lack a mastery of the relevant factual information. More often it's because of poor decisions and/or because they can't get along with their coworkers.

Our sensory lobes integrate relevant incoming and memorized information into a perceptual analysis of the current challenge, which is forwarded to our frontal lobes for decision and response. That process begins in the prefrontal cortex, the repository of the general goals that bias our decisions.

Chapter 2 reported that scientists compare the functions of our prefrontal cortex to the CEO of a corporation, or to the conductor of a symphony orchestra. Located behind our forehead, it's a unique cognitive system in that it's directly interconnected with every distinct functional unit of our brain, and so it plays the key role in integrating information from hundreds of neuronal analysis systems into a preference and decision that are in tune with the general moral/ethical principles that guide our behavior. In effect, the prefrontal cortex determines if the decision is rational and appropriate.

The decision may later prove to be *right or wrong*, but it's a human decision that moves us beyond being a merely reactive *true or false* machine into the universe of adaptive intelligence and the possibility of wisdom.

Our brain's need to differentiate between facts and choices has an intriguing vocational parallel, in that some vocations emphasize precision and truth; others, ambiguity and opinion (although all vocations demand a combination of the two). Consider these emphases as you observe and work with adolescents. An adolescent's orientation toward factual precision (true/false) may suggest such careers as accounting, computer programming, engineering, or medicine. An orientation toward ambiguous belief (right/wrong) may suggest such careers as counseling, politics, sales, or management.

The Development of Our Moral/Ethical Base

During childhood, we tend to assume the moral and ethical beliefs of our parents and other adults who make decisions for us, and we view these more as true/false facts than right/wrong opinions. Further, we consider those who hold other beliefs to be simply incorrect. The situation is similar with the major moral/ethical pronouncements of the religious, political, and other affiliations of a child's family. For example, Christian and Jewish children tend to view the Biblical Ten Commandments as a face-value, true/false document, even though most adults realize that considerable cultural controversy currently exists over the interpretation of "Thou shalt not kill" in such issues as abortion, stem cell research, assisted suicide, capital punishment, and war.

It's important for children to accept their parents' beliefs on moral/ethical issues, because their parents' appropriate or inappropriate beliefs will affect the nature of the sheltering and nurturing that children experience. Such unquestioned acceptance is somewhat analogous to my behavior following a computer malfunction. I simply accept the advice of the service technician about how best to fix the problem, even though several options probably exist. I realize that I lack the knowledge and judgment required to do the repairs myself. Over time, my knowledge of computers and my experience with the service technician may develop to the level that I feel confident enough to veto a suggestion, or even to repair the computer myself—but I've not yet reached that point.

Adolescence triggers the movement toward that sense of personal competence in moral judgment and problem solving. It's based in part on more than a decade of continuous observation of adult interactions, and especially how one's parents interact with each other, their family, friends, neighbors, and strangers. Moral/ethical dichotomies begin to emerge more clearly in the adolescent mind. Behavior thus isn't only about true/false, but it can also fall somewhere along such continua as honest/dishonest, fair/unfair, pleasant/unpleasant, productive/unproductive, responsible/ irresponsible, helpful/unhelpful, to identify a few such dichotomies that can create difficult decisions. Children and adolescents also listen to the disagreements that their parents and other relatives may have about moral and ethical issues. They may even come to realize that their parents and other adult family members are bigoted and/or dishonest. Adolescent maturation thus develops the realization that in adult life the distance between right and wrong is greater than between true and false.

Individual experiences at home, school, and elsewhere gradually evolve into a general moral/ethical sense that guides our life. Sharing toys with a childhood friend leads to sharing tools with an adult neighbor. This developmental process encompasses the values inherent not only in a democratic society, which are taught in school and observed in life, but also in our family's value system. Many parents affiliate with religious and/or other organizations that parallel their beliefs, and such organizations support the family's values. The organization's educational and social programs for young members further inculcate those values. Parents typically hope that such programs will lead to close friendships with children of like-minded parents and even eventually to adult bonding relationships.

Such parental hopes aren't always realized. Adolescence tends to expand friendships beyond family belief systems, and so it's not unusual for adolescents to develop close friendships with peers from families whose values and traditions differ considerably. Some parents view this positively—as an opportunity for their children to expand their awareness of cultural diversity. Other parents view such friendships negatively—as a threat to the maintenance of a cohesive set of family values.

The reality is that children won't spend their adult lives with their birth family. They will bond with a nonkin, and most of their adult friends and coworkers will probably be nonkin. They'll probably also live elsewhere. Our children have to learn how to live and negotiate with people who don't share their family's values.

As suggested earlier, parents get perhaps a dozen years to make the best case they can for the validity of their moral/ethical beliefs. We can give advice to our adolescent children, but we have to realize that they're now on their own exploratory journey to adult autonomy—just as we were—and they'll pick and choose along the way—just as we did. As adults, they'll probably eventually reclaim at least some family values they had laid aside during their adolescence—but they're then adult-chosen and not parent-imposed values. Another option, of course, is that they will abandon their parents' values.

Adolescents also begin to realize that the forces that helped to shape their parents' adolescent moral and ethical values may have changed considerably during the intervening 20 or so years. For example, I indicated earlier that I was a child during the economic depression of the 1930s and an adolescent during World War II and the postwar economic growth period. My experiences were thus considerably different from what our adolescent children observed about war and our nation's economy during the Vietnam War era, and what our adolescent grandchildren are observing now in the Middle East. Each war has been considerably different from the others in terms of its genesis, execution, and effect on upper adolescents.

Similarly, the exponentially escalating advances in science and technology have created a whole new set of cultural issues that the current set of adolescents will confront but that their parents didn't. E-mail and the Internet didn't exist during their parents' adolescence. Nor did our understanding of cloning and stem cells. Nor did suicide bombers. Nor did cell phones. Nor did advanced space explorations. Nor did cable TV. Nor did the extensive outsourcing of manufacturing. Nor did the imaging technologies that are dramatically increasing our understanding of our body and brain. All of these issues and many others have profound moral and ethical implications.

Today's adolescents realize that they may know as much, if not more, about some scientific and technological advances as their parents do. When adolescents think they know as much about something as their parents, they tend not to seek advice from their parents. They attend to favorite teachers. They talk endlessly with peers. They listen to the messages in music and film. In effect, they compare what their parents have been telling them with what others have to say about the same issues.

This takes us back to where we began. It's one thing to know how to do something, and it's quite something else to know whether it's an appropriate thing to do. The frontal lobe systems that process knowing how to do something mature before the systems that determine the appropriateness of the behavior. The anterior cingulate (located between the two hemispheres) is an important frontal lobe participant in the processing of such ambiguous challenges.

An adolescent may thus know how to hack into some-one's computer system but not yet fully understand why it's inappropriate. This suggests that a continuing, but more col-legial, nurturing relationship with parents and teachers is important during adolescence, when these systems mature.

Chapter 1 suggested that nurturing throughout life is most effective if it's continuously grounded in the belief that young people have a birthright to a safe, healthy, and stimu-lating environment that communicates unconditional love. Unconditional love means loving people for who they are rather than for what they do. Parenting and teaching that are based on rewards and punishments send a negative message, in that they create conditions, a kind of economic exchange. Acceptance and love thus emerge as rewards when our children and students do what we request. Young people thus learn to satisfy the desires of others rather than to develop their own personal interests and the collaborative skills that a democratic society requires.

A central tenet of a democratic society is that those who are affected by a decision should directly or indirectly help to make it, whether they're right or wrong in their beliefs. The ballot box and legislative bodies determine the majority deci-sion, and the courts adjudicate the rights of the minority and the aggrieved. A democracy is thus a messy system because of its constant disagreements and negotiations—but would any of us freely choose to live where a monarch efficiently made all the decisions? Many young people live (and misbehave) in such an authoritarian setting—without opportunities to explore the dynamics of moral and ethical behavior beyond following established rules.

Young people will never develop the skills required of citizens in a democratic society if parents and educators don't continually provide them with opportunities to learn how to make moral and ethical decisions and how to evaluate the results of their decisions. Many unilateral decisions that parents and teachers make have excellent potential for teaching young people how to negotiate and collaborate.

But how does one reason with a demanding, immature child or an obstinate adolescent? Take the long view. View any such specific problems within the context of a general strategy to be *in control* rather than to be *controlling;* to teach children how to make, accept, and evaluate decisions rather than to rely on rewards and punishments to ensure compliance.

Parents and teachers don't abrogate their responsibility when they provide many opportunities for participatory decision making, just as democracies don't restrict freedom when they establish laws—provided the citizens understand and accept the logic behind the laws and directly or indirectly participated in the decision. But even then, folks who agree in principle with traffic laws may exceed the speed limit—just as a child who agrees in principle with a parental request may still throw a temper tantrum. Young people have a right to a safe environment, so it's appropriate for an adult to simply make an adult decision if the demand of the child or adolescent is dangerous or inappropriate—but the adult in the transaction should explain the reason behind the decision, to make sure that learning will occur.

Pain helps to identify the nature and location of a body problem, and misbehavior helps to identify the nature and location of an interpersonal problem. Pain and misbehavior are thus diagnostic and not necessarily negative. Adolescence can thus be a painful but not necessarily negative developmental period.

Moving from yelling to telling to explaining to discussing may thus take longer and may not always bring an immediate positive resolution, but it's better in the long run. It will pay off, especially during the decades to come, when parents interact with their children as adults, who will then be thankful that the adults in their early life didn't simply dispense rewards and punishments but, rather, made the effort to teach them how to live a moral and ethical life and how to dispense their own unconditional love along the way.

CHAPTER SIX

Risks and Security

Going Beyond the Known

C hapter 5 looked outward to the development of our moral/ethical sense—the emerging awareness of how our decisions might adversely affect others. This chapter will look inward—to the emerging awareness of how inappropriate and risky decisions might adversely affect our own well-being. The physical abilities and exploratory tendencies of adolescents tend to develop before their judgment matures—and this occurs during a period in which they increasingly make their own decisions. The excitement of risk, their sense of invincibility, and their limited ability to multitask (process several tasks simultaneously) make them vulnerable to physical accidents and social blunders. For example, 6,000 adolescents are killed and 300,000 are injured in automobile accidents in the United States each year.

Although the risky adolescent reach for autonomy is especially worrisome, all humans tend to push the limits of what's biologically possible and culturally appropriate. If the highway speed limit is 70 mph, we check out 71. If adolescents have an 11 p.m. curfew, they'll try for 11:01. The Olympic Games celebrate this seemingly innate drive to increase human performance beyond previous levels—to run a race a fraction of a second faster, to throw a javelin a centimeter farther. This innate drive to strive beyond normality isn't necessarily negative. It has led to the creative innovations and inventions that have shaped human cultures—to tools that boost biological capability, to procedures that improve social interaction, and to aesthetics that enhance and celebrate the ordinary.

We can observe this exploratory drive at all levels of development. Previous chapters indicated that a principal childhood task is to learn how the world works—what's possible and appropriate, what bounces and what breaks. A principal adolescent task is to learn how to respond appropriately to immediate and potential challenges: Must I respond? Can I successfully respond on my own, or should I seek help?

We may wish for the early maturation of such capabilities, but our extended adolescence means that we have more (somewhat sheltered) time to develop and fine-tune the capabilities that we will draw on during several decades of a more challenging adult life. Being a late bloomer thus isn't necessarily negative, despite the turmoil it creates in parents.

OUR BRAIN'S REGULATORY SYSTEMS

Chapter 2 identified several interrelated brain systems that process the cognitive activity that precedes conscious decision and action. An explanation of how these systems function helps to clarify the genesis of risky decisions.

Emotion/Attention

Emotion is a subconscious arousal system that alerts us to potential dangers and opportunities. Think of emotion as a biological thermostat that monitors and responds to variations from normality. Significant sensory variations activate the emotional processes that then activate our conscious attention system. Attention frames foreground out of background by focusing on and identifying the principal elements of the challenge. This awareness activates relevant problem-solving systems that respond to the challenge via either an established routine or a creative solution. Everything we do thus begins with an emotional arousal that activates an attentional focus.

Cognition succinctly described: Emotional arousal drives attentional focus, and focused attention drives problem solving and a behavioral response.

Problems occur if these arousal/focusing systems overrespond or underrespond to stimuli. Most mental illnesses, from autism to schizophrenia, involve emotional or attentional malfunctions—and these systems don't always function efficiently during the brain reorganization that occurs during adolescence.

The renowned neuroscientist Antonio Damasio (2003) differentiates between emotions and feelings. Emotions subconsciously integrate sensory input from within and without and often publicly manifest themselves in facial, body, and speech displays. It's frequently important that we inform others of the nature and severity of the challenge that confronts us. Emotional arousal can lead to conscious feelings that, like mental images and dreams, are hidden from others. Feelings elevate our involvement with the challenge and so play a key role in the subsequent conscious design of our response.

Emotion researchers typically consider fear, anger, disgust, surprise, sadness, and joy to be our primary emotions—and they add other secondary and blended emotions (such as anticipation, tension, pride, and love) to that list.

Curiosity is the ill-understood emotion/attention property that drives childhood and adolescent exploration, and temperament helps to determine the nature and extent of the exploration.

Curiosity

Chapter 2 reported that our right hemisphere (in most people) is organized to analyze and respond to novel challenges and our left hemisphere to familiar challenges. (A small number of people have a reversed hemispheric arrangement, and this doesn't negatively affect their capabilities.) Novel challenges obviously dominate the lives of young people with limited experience, who explore the dynamics and boundaries of a challenge, and then eventually develop successful responses that they activate whenever the challenge recurs.

We tend to lose interest in a discrete challenge once we've successfully solved it. For example, crossword puzzle fans don't erase and redo a successfully completed puzzle. They're more interested in a different crossword puzzle, even though it follows a similar format and may use some of the same words. Similarly, young people lose interest in the video games they've mastered. We all thus seek the novelty of a new challenge, but we typically want it to be somewhat familiar.

Assigning a page of similar homework problems creates the same issue with students who easily master the process or information and thus see no value in doing the rest of the repetitive assignment. Such an assignment creates the opposite problem for students who can't solve the first problem and so see no sense in going on. It's better for a developing adolescent brain that these kinds of repetitive assignments allow for the types of personal decisions adults make in such situations. For example, if you're having difficulty, do as many as you can and then explain the nature of your difficulty. Do as many as you need to do to indicate that you've mastered the process or information.

Play and games provide young people with a nonthreatening, exploratory venue for the types of challenges that they'll also confront in adult life. Play involves informal individual or small-group explorations with a minimal focus on a defined goal and rules.

We eventually wonder how our skills compare with those of others, and so games are organized, rule-bound, and scored comparisons of specific skills exhibited by individual or team competitors who have a clearly defined common goal. Referees are a useful component in games, because players almost always push the edges of what's appropriate. The planning, regulation, and prediction of movement are key brain functions, and so they're also central components of play and games (even in such sedentary games as chess). Collaboration and competition are also similarly central elements of games—and of life.

Children and adolescents spend much time and energy on play and games that challenge them to master developmentally important knowledge and skills—and they frequently have no conscious awareness of the underlying developmental significance of the activity. A three-year-old on a tricycle is beginning an exploration of wheels that will result in an adolescent driver's license. A three-year-old playing a video game is beginning an exploration of computer technology that will eventually lead to surfing the Internet. Basketball players are developing perceptual and motor skills that will later help them to navigate commuter traffic.

The universal childhood and adolescent fascination with scary stories and risky play and games is probably at least partially related to our need to develop and maintain the brain systems that process the important emotion of fear. All emotions involve processing systems that must be developed and maintained for our brain to effectively recognize and respond to dangers and opportunities.

Some of these emotions may not be sufficiently activated in normal life. Play and games frequently and artificially activate fear—and its handmaiden, attention—and this may partly explain our culture's strong and enduring interest in play and games. Note how attention and all the other primary emotions listed above are also central to play and games.

Temperament

Our level of eagerness to explore new challenges is mediated by temperament, a perhaps innate, lifelong emotional response bias to challenges. A person's temperament typically centers somewhere along a continuum between bold/uninhibited and anxious/inhibited, with boldness processed principally in the left hemisphere and anxiousness in the right hemisphere. This makes sense. We're typically more confident about familiar challenges and more anxious about novel challenges.

Temperament is a useful human trait, in that it allows us to quickly and confidently take the first step in response. The bold tend to go forward in curiosity—sensing an opportunity—and the anxious tend to go backward in hesitant concern—sensing danger. Since we frequently follow our developing temperamental bias, we tend to become quite competent with it over time. For example, bold people tend to become skilled at responding boldly. (This is similar to handedness, which develops exceptional competence with the favored hand.)

It's important to realize that people at either end of the temperament continuum can function successfully, even though the bold tend to dominate social situations—sometimes irritatingly so. Our society profits from the strengths of those who are typically either cautious or bold, such as people who run either a conservative or a risky business. Indeed, opposite temperaments often marry each other, and the relationship generally profits from the collaborative strengths of each, if both partners respect the other's temperament, since life confronts us with both dangers and opportunities.

Adolescent friendships similarly may pair temperamental opposites, and team games frequently involve a wide temperamental range in players who have to learn how to function effectively as a collaborative group. Adolescence is a period during which young people determine how best to function within their temperamental bias but without the childhood shielding that their parents had provided when things went awry. A somewhat shy adolescent can thus benefit from the companionship of a friend who is more adventuresome, and vice versa—unless the companion also has a controlling or clinging personality.

From Emotional Arousal to Conscious Decision

Think of being in a state of current contentment (also called mental equilibrium or bodily homeostasis). Our sensory and/or memory systems detect an emotionally arousing stimulus from inside or outside our body—a danger or an opportunity.

What follows is a rapid analysis of the relevant environment and the current state of our body/brain. The basic concerns: What are my current levels of alertness, strength, and energy? Are they such that I'm capable of successfully confronting the challenge—and further, am I motivated to do it? An immature brain would also consider the potential level of adult support in confronting the challenge. Damasio (2003) suggests that an optimistic analysis will activate emotions—such as joy, anticipation, and trust—that signal a joyful body/brain state. Conversely, a pessimistic analysis will activate emotions—such as fear, anger, and grief—that signal a state of sadness. We'll thus move confidently forward toward the resolution of the challenge or we'll warily avoid it.

If the analysis doesn't clearly place us in either category, an uncertain emotion/feeling state results—and surprise, confusion, and anticipation are relevant responses for this state. The traditional fight/flight/freeze categories used to describe behavior in stressful situations thus also describe emotional arousal and its consequent feelings. Adults typically sense this back-and-forth discussion going on in their brain while they're considering such things as a major purchase or a vocational decision. Adolescents frequently supplement this internal dialogue about their version of such issues by discussing the dilemma with friends.

These positive/negative, emotion/feeling states often return after the fact, when we assess the results of our decision. Feelings such as elation and pride follow success, and shame and guilt follow defeat. The emotionally tagged memories of the experience pop up when subsequent similar challenges occur and can bias that analysis.

As suggested above, temperament provides a long-term bias in our level of curiosity and response. Mood, which tends to exist over a shorter period (from a few hours to a few days), can similarly bias the analysis and the resulting emotional state in the direction of the positive or negative mood we're experiencing. We may thus eagerly tackle a problem on Tuesday that we would avoid on Thursday.

Drugs, illness, belief systems, and immature judgment can also bias the accuracy of this analysis and the consequent conscious optimistic or pessimistic feelings that result. We may thus incorrectly feel that we're capable of meeting certain challenges, or vice versa.

What's true of an individual is also observable in social behaviors, such as fluctuating confidence levels in the stock market or in the body language and behavior of sports teams during a game. For example, teams often have confident streaks during which they play very effectively—followed by awkward periods during which they suddenly seem to have lost confidence in themselves. Their body language often communicates their current emotional state and consequent level of play.

The social behavior and risk analysis that preceded the Iraq war similarly paralleled what occurs within a single brain. The national and international debate that was sparked by a proposal for war focused on an assessment of our respective levels of alertness, strength, and energy—but also heavily on our motivation for the enterprise. How much will a war cost? How long will it take? How many will die? What will happen if we don't invade Iraq? What about the aftermath? Should we do it only if other nations join us in a coalition, or should we go it alone? *Should* we do it, even if we *can* do it?

The postwar analysis has been as emotionally driven and perplexing as the prewar analysis. There's thus not much difference between an individual and a social group when it comes to the analysis of a major challenge. Damasio (2003) sees this as an integral part of who we are as human beings—and adolescent awkwardness and poor judgment are simply parts of the developmental process. Autonomy means that we have preferences and we make choices. Sometimes we're wise, and sometimes we're foolish. Ideally we'll learn from both.

THE BIOLOGY OF RISK AND SECURITY

Risk is an element of almost all decisions, and life would probably be boring without at least some of it. Adults fantasize about the financial security they think they'll get from winning a lottery, but the winners aren't necessarily happier—after the initial elation—than they were before they won. Similarly, the appeal of a secure, relaxed retirement disappears for many when they wake up in the morning with nothing to do and no risks to take. Adolescents also take risks in such activities as sports and drama and then discover that the weekend excitement of winning a championship or of having a successful set of performances disappears quickly with the realization that the games or performances are over. It's mundane Monday.

Parents and other adults assume many of the risks that children would otherwise confront. The adolescent reach for autonomy signals an escape from such increasingly irritating adult controls, but often before mature capabilities and judgment develop. We all have our frightening memories. I recall the opportunity that came my way at age 16 when I was learning how to drive. My parents had driven with friends to an event that would last all afternoon, and our car was in the garage. I thought it would be fun to drive around without the constant controlling comments of my father (my driving instructor). I can still recall several heart-thumping events during that escapade. I was afraid and didn't know how to respond. I managed to get the family car home without mishap, but I now know that what I did was unbelievably stupid—but perhaps characteristic of being 16 with an immature impulse control system.

The discussion above suggested that fear is probably our most important emotion. Two brain systems, the **amygdala** and cingulate, play key roles in processing fear.

Amygdala

Innate biological fears are initially processed by our emotional system's amygdala (often called *the fear button*). It's a pair of almond-shaped structures located in the lower front areas of the two temporal lobes. Place a finger on either temple, and the amygdala in that hemisphere will be about an inch and a half (4 cm) into your brain.

If the amygdala receives incoming sensory information that indicates imminent danger (such as a sudden looming movement or a loud noise), it will rapidly signal the nearby hypothalamus to initiate an appropriate automatic primal response (fight, flight, freeze). Fearful information is simultaneously sent into the cingulate area of the frontal lobes for conscious consideration of alternate responses.

The amygdala also adds positive and negative emotional content to the memory of an experience for use in subsequent similar situations, thus playing an important role in the consolidation of long-term memories. Since the amygdala dominates our childhood and early adolescent response to fearful situations, we tend to carry a lot of fearful memories into adolescent and adult life. My solo car experience left me with driving fears that persisted into early adulthood (and in retrospect, those fears probably kept me from many additional ill-advised, impetuous behaviors).

Cingulate

The cingulate reconciles ambiguous challenges. Located on top of the corpus callosum pathway that connects the two hemispheres, it's connected to the prefrontal cortex and to many other brain systems. The cingulate determines the emotional importance (from mere awareness to intense pain) of sensory information sent from the amygdala. It then coordinates the retrieval and analysis of memories of similar challenges or the development of creative alternate responses and transmits this information to the prefrontal cortex for conscious decision and action.

The amygdala thus activates an innate automatic response to an imminent fearful situation, and the cingulate coordinates the conscious preferred response to a nonimminent challenge. In effect, the cingulate helps us to *make up our mind*—and so typically to delay decision. The amygdala dominates childhood response patterns, which are often impulsive and self-centered. The cingulate matures during adolescence, which not surprisingly is characterized by an inconsistent response pattern that ranges from impulsive to thoughtful, from self-centered to altruistic, from instant to deferred gratification.

Think of an adolescent with a new driver's license who makes impulsive and erratic (amygdala-driven) driving decisions, but whose experienced (cingulate-driven) skateboard movements are planned and controlled.

Molecular Messengers

Information and decisions zip around in our brain through the actions of more than 50 different kinds of neurotransmitters, which either activate or inhibit the actions of other neurons within a neural network. Although many neurotransmitters may be involved in a given cognitive process, dopamine is a key neurotransmitter for understanding risky adolescent behavior.

Dopamine is synthesized in a small brain stem area called the **substantia nigra** and is then transported into the frontal lobes and other areas, where it plays a key role in the regulation of emotional arousal, attentional focus, decision making, and behavior. Appendix A explains how neurons and neurotransmitters function, and Chapter 7 will discuss how dopamine and other neurotransmitters are involved in drug use.

Since it's important to remember past successes and failures when we confront repeated challenges, our brain has a dopamine-mediated pleasure-and-reward system that chalks up successes and encourages repetition of successful behaviors. The dopamine levels in this circuitry are high in childhood, when it's especially important to know what works, and they decline through adolescence into adulthood as we develop an increasing repertoire of successful responses and a consequent sense of efficient competence.

Combine the increased adolescent freedom from close adult supervision with a still very active pleasure-and-reward system, and the typical result is an adolescent who looks for thrills and takes risks. The adolescent tank is full of high-octane dopamine.

Our innate curiosity seeks novelty, and so adolescence is a period of intense, dopamine-fueled exploration. The adolescent tendency to reject whatever conventional adults are doing in order try out something new makes sense to them, since they believe that adults can't give credible advice on something they can't comprehend and aren't experiencing.

ADULTS AND ADOLESCENT RISKS

Would that a simple effective strategy existed for parents and educators to mediate adolescent risk taking! Chapter 1 suggested that the negative results of childhood risk taking tend to be less severe than adolescent risk taking—a bruised leg or a temporary squabble among friends compared to a serious automobile accident or a pregnancy. So the stakes have increased.

It perhaps sounds banal, but the best ways to help adolescents avoid risky behavior are to *be a good role model* and to *continue the conversation* throughout adolescence, as difficult as this may be. It's difficult for adolescents to talk person-to-person with their parents and other adults, because they're discovering that the heroic role model figures they knew in childhood aren't quite that heroic. It's similarly difficult for parents to talk person-to-person with their adolescent because the compliant child they once knew isn't quite as compliant. So it's a continuation of the childhood conversation, but the conversation changes when adults mentor adolescents.

Adolescent frontal lobes may not be mature, but they're developing—and parents can enhance that development by elevating the conversation to the rational level characteristic of adult discussion, even if it doesn't always work. Adults want to know why they should or shouldn't do something, and an adolescent who's rationally beginning to comprehend and compare alternatives wants the same kind of explanation. "Because I said so" doesn't really enhance that developmental process.

Adolescents need to know the cost of risks. For example, it's important to explain in a rational, nonjudgmental manner, at a noncrisis time, what happens to the family's car insurance costs when an adolescent drives and what happens to the cost when the adolescent has an accident or is cited. They can do the math. If they have minimum-wage service jobs, they can figure out the cost of risky decisions in terms of the number of compensatory hours they might have to work. The situation is similar with homeowner's insurance and partying when parents aren't home—and many other potentially risky behaviors. Autonomy isn't free.

One of our preschool grandchildren was harassing her parents about something she wanted them to buy her. When they told her they couldn't afford it, her solution was simple: Go to the bank and take it out of the wall.

Adolescents who begin to take on mature responsibilities through part-time jobs, school activities (such as on a newspaper staff or athletic team), or volunteer activity in the community will inevitably observe the negative effects of poor judgment from the prospective of someone who has to clean up the mess it caused.

Unconditional love doesn't equate to license. It's important for parents and educators to create an adolescent environment that reduces risky behavior, but that does it in a manner appropriate to the development of an autonomous brain. But still, it's always appropriate to just say *no* when saying *no* is appropriate. For example, we often say *no* to persistent telemarketers, so it's similarly appropriate to say *no* to an adolescent's persistent cell phone request to attend a party that promises many more minuses than positives.

CHAPTER SEVEN

Technology and Drugs

Going Beyond Nature

O ur body and brain are excellent, but not perfect. Biological perfection would allow us to successfully confront any challenge and extend our life span for decades beyond its current range. We would then need a stronger skeletal structure, organs that aren't susceptible to debilitating maladies, an enhanced immune system, and a brain and motor system that could run endlessly. But imagine the tremendous biological cost of the basic, backup, and regenerative systems that such an arrangement would require.

Organisms develop regulatory and protective systems suitable for the environment they inhabit and a normative life span that allows them to reproduce and nurture juvenile offspring (if the species requires such nurturing). The young thus may die, but the old must die to maintain the vibrancy of a species and the environment it inhabits. An ecologically healthy environment requires a predator/prey balance among its competing organisms. A single dominant species will eventually deplete the organic nutrients it needs to survive.

Humans are ecologically expensive. We now typically live well beyond our childrearing years, and we've populated (perhaps overpopulated) the entire world. We've already rid the world of many plant and animal species that competed with our real and imagined needs—and we're paving over topsoil at an alarming rate.

Adolescence begins a rapid increase in human body/brain capabilities. Since we're a social species, the looming productive and reproductive adult years implicitly signal to adolescents that they will have to go well beyond what biology has allocated for their individual survival in order to also directly and indirectly nurture the lives of others. As their frontal lobes mature into an awareness of the daunting cultural task that confronts them, most adolescents combine creativity with realism to determine how best to identify and capitalize on their capabilities and reduce the negative impact of their limitations. They'll get help from two sources.

We cope with our biological limitations through (1) an innate stress response that temporarily elevates our biological response capabilities beyond normal levels and (2) technologies (from medications to microphones) that compensate for our biological limitations and extend our biological capabilities.

BIOLOGICAL STRESS

Chapters 2 and 6 indicated that an imminent danger or opportunity often results in a reflexive stress response that is commonly called fight/flight/freeze. To simplify a complex chain of events, our sensory awareness of the current challenge is sent to the amygdala, which activates the hypothalamus, which activates the **pituitary gland,** which activates the **adrenal glands,** which secrete stress hormones (such as **cortisol**) into the bloodstream. Our heart rate increases to move needed nutrients and hormones rapidly throughout our body and brain in order to raise or reduce the response capabilities of many complementary systems. For example, energy levels are increased in the large muscle groups that execute fight/flight behaviors but are decreased in low-priority muscle groups (such as the stomach) and in our immune system—digestion and infection being immediately less important than getting out of the way of an unexpected, rapidly approaching car.

Cortisol, which enhances rapid fight/flight behaviors during a stress response, inhibits the reflective thought processes that delay response. This might seem strange until we realize that although reflective thought is a good idea when purchasing a car, it's not necessarily useful when trying to get out of the way of a rapidly approaching car. We can all recall examples of impulsive responses we've made during stressful situations that later proved to be foolish. The point of a stress response is to quickly do whatever it takes to remain alive and worry later about the details. Stress thus activates a limited repertoire of assertive, general-purpose responses, such as "move quickly away from danger."

Worse, the chronic activation of reflexive stress responses can negatively affect the robustness of our reflective thought processes. Stress emerged as a short-term, high-octane response system for dealing with imminent, survival-level physical challenges. Its chronic inappropriate activation wears out key body/brain response systems. Many of the challenges we confront today are social or cultural in nature. It's foolish to activate a high-octane stress response over a social issue that could be better resolved through negotiation or over a problem that has no real solution.

Adolescents are quite vulnerable to stress responses because their frontal lobe response systems aren't mature and their parents aren't sheltering them from problems as much as they did during childhood. Adolescents thus tend to activate a primal stress response in social situations that would probably be more satisfactorily resolved if they counted to 10 before responding. Unfortunately, arguing and fighting occur far too often among adolescents because of the immaturity of all involved.

It's important to note, however, that our stress response is an important part of our adaptive capabilities. It automatically and appropriately activates during physically dangerous situations, such as when skiing or learning to drive. When the danger passes, the stress system shuts down and normal processes resume. Hans Selye, the scientist who discovered stress, once said that the only organisms he knew of that didn't experience stress were dead people and vegetables. Stress is like season-ings—a little bit is generally good; a whole lot isn't.

Parents and schools should help adolescents develop the cognitive systems that can reflectively override inappropri-ately activated, reflexive stress responses. Role-playing and simulation activities in school allow students to observe, rehearse, and debrief situations that could escalate seriously in real life. Sports and other extracurricular activities similarly place adolescents into situations in which they have to deal with adversity. They learn to accept the incorrect call of a ref-eree or the rejection of their ideas by others on a committee, even when they're unhappy about it.

Middle school programs that teach babysitting skills pre-pare adolescents for otherwise stressful situations that might occur and for the appropriate care of children they may even-tually have. Programs that teach friendship skills and obliga-tions similarly prepare adolescents for reflective responses to potentially stressful social problems.

Involving adolescents in the process of making family decisions demonstrates how adults rationally contemplate alternatives, delay decisions if additional time is needed, and negotiate compromise when necessary. The effort parents expend in developing such competence pays big dividends when adolescents become adults and don't come home for parental intervention and financial aid in the resolution of their personal problems.

TECHNOLOGICAL ENHANCEMENT

We have a curious, inventive brain. Curiosity may have killed the cat, but it led us to develop technologies that shore up our biological limitations and extend our normal capabilities. We saw birds fly and fish swim, and we thought them pretty neat ideas.

Similarly, our 10-octave auditory range is narrower than that of many animals. Our curiosity about sound patterns beyond our biological range thus led to the invention of the oscilloscope, which can transduce sounds we can't hear into oscillating visual patterns that we can mentally comprehend. Telescopes and microscopes similarly extend our visual range.

Further, our brain is much better at estimation than precision when confronted with large quantities. We thus invented arithmetic algorithms and calculators to ensure precision. Our imprecise memory led to telephone books, tape recorders, and many other forms of external memory.

We tend to think of technology principally in machine terms—bridges and bicycles. Screwdrivers and knives are technological extensions of our fingernails; tweezers and pliers, of our fingers. Technology is actually any external organization of time, space, and/or energy that enhances human life or compensates for biological limitations. A *next available teller* line in a bank is thus a time-enhancement and frustration-reduction technology, and medications are a chemical compensatory technology.

Drugs are included in this chapter because they are a form of technology. They compensate for biological limitations and so allow us to consciously override the normal functioning of body systems. Drugs can keep us awake when we would otherwise fall asleep, and vice versa. Drugs can reduce pain and increase euphoria. They can speed up and slow down body processes. It's thus useful for drug education programs to consider drugs an important branch of technology.

We can almost think of technology as a layer of cortex on the outside of our skull, since technologies do many of the same things that the interior cortex does: process sensory input and motor output, remember/analyze/organize information, make and execute decisions. Our brain's range in these actions is finite. Technology is potentially infinite.

The electronic revolution of the past quarter century led to the development of many computerized technologies that mystify older but not younger people. Adults tend to develop a comfort level around familiar technologies and expect new technologies to be user-friendly—to adapt to them rather than the other way around. Young people aren't as committed to current technologies, and so they adapt more easily to the new developments. They are thus typically way ahead of older people in their understanding and skillful use of complex new technologies, such as computers.

Adults rather than students run schools, so although the number of school computers is now increasing, it's probably correct to say that the school was the last pencil-driven institution in our society.

Since adolescence is a period during which we weaken family bonds in order to seek bonding elsewhere, it's not surprising that adolescents have always embraced new technologies that enhance exploration and communication beyond home and family boundaries. The automobile, films, and TV were a boon to 20th-century adolescents. New forms of electronic media and mass media, such as cell phones, e-mail, and blogs, are similarly central to early-21st-century adolescent exploration and communication and so will be the focus of this discussion.

A definition is probably in order. The term *mass media* refers to any communicative form that is broadly distributed to anyone who wants it and, in some cases, can pay for it. It thus includes not only the various forms of print and electronic media but also museums, churches, parades, concerts, and sports events. So an e-mail message is a private communication, but it becomes mass media if it's also sent to one's entire mailing list and is then exponentially sent on via other mailing lists.

Adults are frequently fearful that contemporary electronic mass media (such as video games, films, TV, computers, and the Internet) provoke culturally inappropriate behavior and reduce problem-solving abilities in young people. The principal criticisms have focused on content rather than on the cognitive demands that such media make on the players/viewers. Johnson (2005) and others now question that belief on the basis of recent research.

It's important to realize that popular culture isn't high culture, so it shouldn't be compared to it. Video games and popular TV programs don't broaden intellectual horizons—and neither do golf, fishing, crossword puzzles, and card playing. What all such activities have in common is that they increase knowledge and/or problem-solving abilities within specific parameters of interest to the players.

Book reading, an activity that electronic media critics consider more intellectually stimulating than video games, is basically the passive observation of someone else's thought processes. The reader tries to predict what will occur but has no control over the narrative flow (and this is also the case with those who observe TV programs and films).

Video Games

Conversely, a person who is playing a complex contemporary video game must first determine the purpose and rules of the game (which typically aren't provided) and then continually make decisions that can actually alter the course of the game—but always with the basic presumed goal of the game in mind. The content of a video game is thus secondary to the thought processes involved in planning and executing game movements and in predicting the movements of the video game and one's opponent. The same things would be true of a chess or tennis match, or even of fishing. Chapter 2 suggested that the planning, regulation, and prediction of movements are the central properties of our brain.

Most games (including video games) aren't really pleasurable when complex challenges loom—third and long in football, the loss of a queen in chess. But such situations get the juices flowing in players who seek challenge within the game. Players must quickly and successfully draw on related previous strategies, or make creative, risky decisions in order to stay in the game, and this enhances their problem-solving abilities within that setting.

A game must thus have a strong emotional attraction that will maintain the effort the game requires. Competition, violence, and sexuality are innately arousing emotionally, and so it's not surprising that they're explicit (or at least implicit) in many games and media narratives. Indeed, even revered childhood fairy tales contain violent and sexual themes. Hansel and Gretel worried about getting baked in an oven, and a princess kissed a frog in *The Frog Prince*. How kinky can a children's fairy tale get?

The challenge and complexity of the most popular newer video games are such that they don't need a heavy dose of violence and sexuality to initiate and maintain interest. For example, the immensely popular *SimCity* challenges the player to design a complex metropolis, and the continually popular but more abstract *Tetris* forces the player to quickly make decisions about the placement of geometric shapes.

Video games (and other games, such as hockey and football) that require rapid, aggressive responses to potentially dangerous situations will obviously strengthen the neural circuitry that processes similar decisions. It's problematic, though, whether this increased capability generally makes the player more aggressive in the real world. Current commentary on this issue is based more on opinion than on solid research. It's very difficult to do credible cause-and-effect research on this issue.

I suspect that many adults who decry the violence and sexuality that they believe are endemic in video games watch TV shows and sports that contain violent and sexual content—oblivious to the inconsistency between their beliefs and behavior.

TV and Films

Like readers, viewers of projected media don't control or even affect the narrative flow. They will often guess the answers in TV quiz shows, critique the flow of reality shows and contests, call in to talk shows, and discuss the shows and films they've seen, but TV and films are much more passive than video games. We sit forward for video games and sit back for TV and films.

Johnson (2005) suggests that we should differentiate between intelligent films and TV programs and those that force us to be intelligent (and we could say the same thing of books). Intelligent productions go beyond clichés and provide stimulating plots and witty dialogue. The basic intelligence portrayed thus exists within the people on the screen (or in the book) and not within the viewers.

Conversely, the plots and subplots of many contemporary TV shows and films that appeal to adolescents make strong intellectual demands. They are complex and convoluted, omit information the viewer must insert, don't clearly differentiate between foreground and background, and require advanced cultural knowledge. *Seinfeld* was a TV show about nothing significant that drew a large audience who were stimulated by the show's intellectual demands. For example, it would set up a joke in one episode and provide the punch line several episodes later, without repeating the setup. A good novel similarly requires readers to hold and mentally manipulate multiple subplots.

The Internet

The networking that permeates the Internet makes it potentially the most intellectually challenging of the new media forms, and probably also the most dangerous. Consider what e-mail, Web sites, and search engines could do five years ago and what they can do now. Blogs didn't even exist. Project ahead five years, and it's obvious that many new interactive forms will emerge that will force sophisticated thought.

As indicated in Chapter 4, print media editors and publishers typically check sources to ensure credibility. A student who cites a print source in a course paper is thus more certain of its credibility than a student who clips information off a Web site. The Internet is a free-for-all, and so unfortunately, sexual predators, con artists, and folks who want to spread misinformation can act as easily as those who behave responsibly. It takes intelligence to stay one step ahead of Internet schlock and treachery.

Pac-Man and *Donkey Kong* almost defined the video game genre a half generation ago, and other forms of electronic media have similarly exploded within our culture. We won't return to what was. Electronic media are obviously scary for parents and educators, because they are increasingly open to abuse. The increased power and portability of equipment means that adolescents can technologically access information that they're not biologically ready to handle.

The challenge for parents and educators is to prepare the next generation for the natural and electronic environments in which they will live. A continually increasing number of adults grew up in the electronic age and so are personally familiar with the impact that new forms of mass media have on young people. The conventional wisdom that video game addicts are mostly children and adolescents isn't true. Many avid gamers are adults.

Adults who mentor adolescents today realize that they must explore the current electronic environments—play the video games, watch the TV programs, and surf the Internet sites. It's not an onerous challenge, since electronic media that many consider culturally negative can actually be intellectually and psychologically positive—and thus well worth the family and classroom conversations they can spark.

But this will happen only if we help adolescents understand that both print and electronic media provide a wide range of quality—from the totally terrible to the sublimely superb. We must always consider the context and credibility of any form of mass media. A media artifact can provide an honest, balanced treatment of an issue, or it can present a single perspective. Either is appropriate as long as the intent is clearly expressed and the target audience is sufficiently mature to realize it. A negative and regrettably frequent example would be irresponsible, fear-mongering news or commentary that implies that a rare but emotionally charged incident is common. It's as if such folks consider credible data to be the plural of an incredible anecdote—and they get away with it far too often.

If adolescent consumers of mass media perceive a distorted depiction as real and normal, mass media do a disservice. Conversely, if adolescents perceive distorted depictions as aberrant, the distortion can actually help to develop rational capabilities. That's because those who hope to understand the normative center of a phenomenon must also know about its outer reaches—and mass media often provide a useful metaphoric format for observing the outer reaches of something without actually experiencing it (such as the depicted escape from a dangerous situation that we might actually confront, or an obviously satirical depiction of a news event).

So perhaps it's not what mass media bring to an adolescent that's most important, but rather what the adolescent brings to the mass media. Adolescents who mature in a secure home and school with adults who explore all the dimensions of humanity in an unhurried, accepting atmosphere can probably handle most mass media without psychological damage. They will tend to look deeper than the surface of depicted issues. They will probably also engage in extended conversations about the issue with real people. They will thus develop the balance that permits them to be a part of the real and mass-media worlds—but also to stand apart from them when it's appropriate.

Drug Support

Sticks were probably among the first tools that we humans used in our long ascent to the complex technologies that extend our biological capabilities and compensate for our limitations. The leaves or fruit of the bush that supplied the stick may also have provided the first drugs. Then as now, humans used drugs because they allow us to do things we otherwise couldn't do as easily, if at all.

The concept of *drug* is somewhat nebulous in that its basic definition—a chemical agent that in small amounts can significantly modify the way a body/brain functions—could include food, seasonings, and poison as well as heroin, prescription drugs, alcohol, and aspirin.

Drugs have been integral to human life for millennia, but until relatively recently, we didn't know much about what they were or how they created their effects. Consequently, drugs took on a mystical character. People spoke of magic mushrooms and reefer madness. Wine was the nectar of the gods. Drugs were incorporated into religious ceremonies and holiday celebrations. Experiences with drugs ranged from exciting to fearful, from helpful to destructive.

Drug education programs emerged out of this general lack of understanding of the psychobiology of drugs, and so a strong moral tone dominated: Don't use drugs because they're harmful. Schools spoke of their "drug and alcohol program" (as if alcohol was something other than a drug) or of having a drug-free campus (as if the coffeepots and soda machines were completely free of drugs).

Drug education is important, because people who use psychoactive drugs typically begin during adolescence—and not surprisingly with alcohol, nicotine, and/or marijuana. They're available, and they appeal to adolescents (despite their negative effects) because they can compensate for real and imagined adolescent concerns. All three have multiple effects, depending on dosage and other factors, but alcohol reduces social inhibitions and so enhances conversation. Nicotine reduces fatigue and so increases mental alertness. Marijuana primes a euphoric, mellowed-out state by enhancing relaxation and reducing inhibitions. All can thus provide welcome support for stressed-out adolescents who are unsure of their social competence and are increasingly wary of adult controls in their life.

The downside is that the adolescent brain is very sensitive to pleasure and reward, but its impulse control systems aren't yet mature. Adolescents are thus vulnerable to exploration with highly rewarding drugs—and alcohol and other psychoactive drugs affect adolescent brain development and function much more than they affect an adult brain.

About 50 percent of the adolescents who begin drinking before the age of 14 become alcohol-dependent at some point in their lives, compared to about 10 percent of those who wait until at least age 21 before they begin to drink. Adolescent alcohol use negatively affects memory, attention, and spatial/ motor skills that are important in school (and alcohol-fueled memory impairment isn't surprising to anyone who couldn't remember what occurred during a drinking spree). The emerging information on the negative long-term effects of adolescent alcohol use are disquieting, and especially in the maturation of the frontal lobes and hippocampus, which plays a key role in memory.

Adults are appropriately concerned about the negative impact of such drugs as methamphetamine, cocaine, heroin, and ecstasy, but it's important to remember that the seemingly milder drugs also pose serious risks. The inappropriate sharing of prescription drugs among adolescents is another growing problem. Medications prescribed for adolescents with such illnesses as attention deficit disorder (ADD) should not be experimentally shared with friends—but they are.

Since our knowledge of the biochemistry and effects of drugs has now dramatically increased, school drug education programs should go beyond the moral overtones and end effects of drug use to a stronger focus on clear explanations of what drugs are, how they and their addictive properties work, and how to live intelligently with them. The explanation below is an example of the kind of nontechnical information that teachers can adapt to adolescent comprehension. This shift, which is already occurring, will certainly rekindle the same argument used against sex education programs: If you teach students about sexuality (drugs), they will become sexually active (use drugs). Well, we've been teaching algebra to students for centuries and they still don't rush out and do algebra.

Psychoactive Drugs: A Primer

Neurotransmitter molecules produced within a *sending* neuron pass information to a *receiving* neuron at the synapse (the narrow gap between two neurons). The complementary shapes of the neurotransmitter and the receptor on the postsynaptic neuron allow them to bind (somewhat like a key and lock) and then to pass and receive chemical information.

The synapse is an area of constant molecular activity that would be chaotic without its simple molecular binding system. Think of a hotel with many people constantly entering, milling about, and leaving. Key codes and shapes ensure the correct match of hotel guests to rooms. The front part of the key contains the room's *address* and the back part the *information*—the patron holding it who can use it to enter the assigned room. Anyone who holds the key or its duplicate has access to the room.

Psychoactive drugs are herbal or synthetic molecules that sufficiently resemble the molecules involved in brain processes to attach to the appropriate receptors (Appendix A provides examples). A psychoactive drug molecule enters our body through respiration, digestion, or injection; moves into our brain via the bloodstream; and then enters into a synaptic area. Like a duplicate key, the drug uses its similar shape and chemical properties to attach to a presynaptic or postsynaptic receptor, and to alter one of a variety of chemical actions that can occur in a synapse. For example, it can mimic the actions of a neurotransmitter that is typically released into the synapse; or it can alter the rate and quantity of neurotransmitter release, the shape and number of receptors, the strength of the action, or the ability of the presynaptic neuron to reuse its neurotransmitters.

The actions of psychoactive drugs can thus positively or negatively affect normal brain activity. Because the shape and chemical properties of drugs mimic those of useful brain molecules, drugs can obviously have positive effects, as exemplified by the widespread use of potentially dangerous drugs. Further, drugs can stabilize the imbalances in neurotransmitter distribution experienced by many people. (For example, lithium stabilizes norepinephrine distribution patterns in people suffering from bipolar affective disorder.)

Because drugs flood into the synapses of a brain area via the bloodstream rather than through the carefully regulated axon terminals of interrelated neurons, their heavy concentration and unregulated movements in and out of synapses can also negatively affect us—within the immediate brain region and in other parts of our body/brain. Thus, the caffeine that keeps us awake (and perhaps alive) during the final segment of a long, late drive home will also probably delay our desired sleep because the effects of caffeine persist over three hours.

The small amount of alcohol that initially released our inhibitions in a social setting can, with increased consumption, trigger inappropriate behavior and uncoordinated movements. The morphine that reduces pain and enhances euphoria in addicts also reduces our brain's production of its own opiates and so extends the addiction.

So psychoactive drugs are both helpful and harmful and almost always require a trade-off between the two. To maintain a qualitative life, our conscious brain must carefully control its drug selection and dosage (and by extension, its food selection and quantity), just as its unconscious partners in our skull and glands carefully control the production and distribution of neurotransmitters and hormones.

The brain mechanisms that respond to our environment's challenges mature during childhood and adolescence. Extensive drug use during this period can adversely affect this maturation, because drugs alter our brain's natural perception of and response to the environment. Thus, one drug may help keep us awake so that we can complete a task by its deadline, but another drug could negatively affect maturing neural networks that are critical to the problem-solving task. Drugs are neither good nor bad per se. They are chemical technologies that positively and negatively affect the processing effectiveness of our biological brain.

An effective drug education program should therefore help students learn how to use their own biological resources to solve a problem and to use drugs only when that assistance is essential to maintaining an acceptable quality of life—realizing even then that drugs have addictive properties that can reduce our ability to control their use.

Students need this kind of factual, nonmoralizing information in drug education programs so that they can learn to make informed conscious choices about what they put into their bodies and brains. They similarly must understand the nature and appropriate use of all other technologies if they are to live their adult lives in harmony with the organic, inorganic, and electronic environments we all now share.

CHAPTER EIGHT

The Arts and Humanities

Going Beyond Reality

C hapter 7 discussed various technologies we've developed to compensate for our biological limitations and enhance our biological capabilities. The arts and humanities take us one step further and insert aesthetics into human life, and especially into its central function of movement. They allow us to go beyond mere survival—to live and move with style and grace. The arts enhance objects, places, events, and our cognitive processes. The humanities enhance reflections on our life experiences and cultural beliefs.

The arts and humanities are thus a celebration of the ordinary, in that they transform the ordinary into something that's aesthetically extraordinary. What's intriguing about the arts and humanities is that they stimulate those who do them and also those who observe others do them. People who don't play an instrument attend concerts. People who don't paint appreciate paintings. People who don't write novels read them. The arts and humanities are a totally win/win situation culturally, in that both the doers and the observers discover something about the further reaches of being human.

Chapter 6 suggested that emotional arousal drives attentional focus, and focused attention drives problem solving and behavioral response. Since emotion and attention are prerequisites to thought and action, the arts and humanities may have become significant elements of human life because they activate the emotional and attentional systems of both the doers and observers. The pleasurable, stimulating nature of the arts and humanities has made them ubiquitous in human life, and this helps to maintain the tenor and robustness of our emotion/attention systems during down periods, when we're not confronting survival challenges. When you think about it, folks typically don't stop to look at the paintings when rabid wolves are chasing them through a museum!

The arts and humanities are especially significant in the lives of adolescents who are shaping their personal and social identities—seeking to move with style and grace from ordinary to extraordinary. They and their maturing cognitive systems benefit from the artistic expressions of others and also from their own artistic explorations.

Considerable archaeological evidence exists that the arts were important to human life from the earliest times. For example, it took much time and effort to make the strings of beads discovered in ancient sites, given the primitive jewelry-making technology available at the time. Jewelry is still expensive, in that buying equally nonfunctional contemporary strings of beads requires the income from many working hours. What's the point of a string of beads? Why did the ancients also decorate their tools and clothing? And while we're at it, what's the point of song and dance and narrative and drama?

ADORNMENT

Personal adornment of the six-pound, 20-square-foot, two-layer mantle of skin that covers our body seems to have always been important—and it's very important to contemporary adolescents, who want to be recognized as adolescents, but who also want to stand out in a crowd of other adolescents. Skin is skin, but tattoos, cosmetics, hairstyles, clothing, and jewelry can distinguish people and thus express both one's individual identity and group membership.

The outer, visible parts of our skin, hair, nails, and teeth are all dead tissue, but we expend inordinate time and energy trying to make them look alive and attractive. Perhaps it's the mortician and artist within us. Entire industries are dedicated to this cosmetic compulsion to attract the attention of others by adorning and manipulating dead tissue—to no avail. What others see of our body's biological covering is dead. Life pulsates within.

Still, we can infer much about the race, gender, state of health, approximate age, occupation, marital status, habits, and values of people by simply observing their head and hands, the two body parts we tend to leave uncovered. We can infer even more from clothing, the principal (technological) extension of our skin. Like our skin's outer layer of dead epidermal cells, clothing is made of dead material (cotton, wool, leather, and chemical synthetics). Because clothing and jewelry provide a far more flexible communicative format than skin, we can use this second *skin* layer to communicate even more of what we consider the real person hidden within our brains and bodies. For example, military people in full uniform symbolically drape their entire professional biographies on their bodies.

Social categorization can arise out of such surface communication—the hurt that comes from racism and sexism, the help that comes from recognizing a police officer when we need one. Adolescents have long sought to distance themselves from children and adults through distinctive dress and manner that signal not only adolescence but also their individuality. Adolescents thus want their clothing and other adornment to set them apart, but not too far apart.

It's not a huge conceptual leap to go from body adornment to painting on stretched canvas to decorating a room to designing a house. We can also conceptually leap from hairstyling to sculpture, from braids to woven cloth, from dangling earrings to mobiles. The visual arts began with a personal canvas, and then they went everywhere. Imagine a human visual system that had to function within a bland world devoid of the visual arts. The plants and birds would shame us with their visual displays. And may further shame be heaped upon schools that eliminate instruction in the visual arts.

Language, Music, and Dance

Chapters 2 and 4 reported that our upright stance and consequent narrow female birth canal led to helpless infants with a brain one third its adult size, and so to a long, dependent maturation during which children and adolescents gradually learn how to live successfully within our complex culture. Our upright stance also freed our arms and hands to carry and cuddle, to gesture, and to fashion in ways that helped to define human life and art. Innate parent/child bonding is thus essential to a successful extended maturation.

The mutual love between parents and child is initially expressed through emotionally charged melodic interactions and rhythmic, imitative behaviors that are innately mediated by mirror neurons. These simple beginnings lead to conscious adult expressions of love and the arts—and to ceremonial rituals, such as weddings and funerals, that meld emotional human bonding with artistic elaboration.

This complex process begins simply—with a symbiotic unspoken agreement between child and mother that says, "I'll reduce the pressure within your breast if you'll fill my empty stomach." Other universally practiced child/parent behaviors strengthen this close relationship. For example, *motherese* is the term commonly used for the high-pitched, exaggerated, repetitive, melodic communication format that engages infants' attention, even though they initially don't understand the words we use.

It introduces a baby to the verbal and musical communication forms and rhythms that dominate human life. The joy that infants typically express encourages parents to continue *motherese* until the child's related verbal abilities begin to emerge. But music was there first, and we often return to music at times when words alone fail us.

To place this important communicative interaction into context, primates and other social animals typically communicate through (1) grooming (caressing in humans), a form of personal tactile interaction that involves direct body stimulation; and (2) an auditory social signaling system that communicates information about current dangers, opportunities, and relationships.

Human languages typically use about four dozen phonemes, about the same number of signaling sounds that some primates have. The difference is that a single innate primate signal isn't combined with other signals, but rather communicates a complete important idea (such as the nature and location of food or danger).

Conversely, learned human language strings combinations of meaningless phonemes into sound sequences that become hundreds of thousands of meaningful words, and strings those into word sequences that become sentences and stories that are even more complex. The vast amount of information in human language is thus not coded into the relatively few sounds (and letters), but rather into the sequence of the sounds and letters and the length of the information sequence (do, dog, god, good, and so on).

Music and numbers function similarly. Just 12 scale tones and 10 digits can create incredibly complex forms of musical and mathematical information, because the meaning is similarly coded into the sequence and length of the information chain, and not into the elements themselves. It's a marvelously simple system for processing complex cognitive information.

What's intriguing is that genetic communication uses a similar sequential coding mechanism. The nucleus of a cell is composed principally of a long, ladder-shaped, twisted molecule called deoxyribonucleic acid, or DNA. Some 30,000 human DNA segments called genes regulate cell processes and initiate the assembly of proteins, the basic cellular building blocks of our body. A gene contains the coded directions for assembling a protein out of a unique sequential combination of the 20 different kinds of amino acids that cell bodies contain.

Only 20 amino acids are needed to assemble an infinite number of proteins, for the same reason that only 26 alphabetic letters are needed to construct the some 500,000 words in the English language. The sequence of amino acids spelled out in the gene determines a protein's shape and thus its genetic information.

So at conception, parents combine their genetic sequences to tell their embryonic child how to develop its body (nose placement, skin color, gender, and so on), and then when the child is born, the parents and other adults use language and musical sequences to tell the child how to live within our culture. It's beautifully mind-boggling.

Articulate speech compresses an extended thought into a stream of rapidly moving phonemic sounds that transmit information. The spoken message identifies key objects (nouns) and events (verbs) that are then clarified by adjectives and adverbs and syntactically positioned by prepositions and conjunctions. Variations in volume and tone are typically reduced in order to increase the flow of information.

Conversely, song communicates how we feel about a unit of information. Song communicates a short but emotionally strong message of love and hate, of commitment and alienation, of opportunity and danger, by slowing down the flow of the message (extending the vowels, repeating phrases). This permits the singer to use such musical properties as melody, rhythm, volume, timbre, and instrumental accompaniment to insert powerful emotional overtones into such primal messages as "I love you" or "I reject war" or "Don't abandon me." Such emotional overtones are much more difficult to insert into speech—adjectives and adverbs typically being a poor substitute for musical properties. As Marshall McLuhan once put it, "Song is the slowing down of speech in order to savor nuance."

It's intriguing that children spend much of the first 10 years of their lives mastering the vocabulary and syntax of oral and written language—the knowledge and skills they must develop in order to communicate effectively with others about complex personal and cultural phenomena.

Conversely, adolescence is probably the single decade in our lifetime during which we're most fascinated by music. It's not surprising that this is also the time during which we develop our personal and social identity, our likes and dislikes.

We thus have two complementary languages. Speech helps us to rapidly and articulately communicate a lot of information to everyone. Song helps us to slowly and melodically communicate personal feelings, beliefs, and commitments to those who mean the most to us. Reading about the organization and development of the United States isn't the same experience as listening to someone singing *America the Beautiful*.

Each generation seems to develop its own musical forms. Contemporary adolescent music is rhythmic, conversational, and improvisational—somewhat related to the emerging pulsating cell phone, e-mail, and blog communication formats that seem increasingly central to adolescent life. Adolescence is often also characterized as a period of verbal reductionism— single-word responses to parental queries that perhaps reduce the word count in order to savor the nuances of muttering and grunts.

It's important for young people to be grounded in the grammatical structures that enhance verbal communication, and it's equally important for them to become grounded in the *grammar* of music. Instructional programs that teach instrumental music and choral singing are examples of how to provide children with musical skills and a sense of the structure and aesthetics of music before they embark on their musically driven adolescent search for personal and social identity. Without such instruction, adolescent music becomes improvisational variations on an unknown theme. There's nothing wrong with musical noodling, but there's something right about helping young people to understand the underlying structure and dynamics of music.

The continuing decline of formal K–12 musical instruction in schools is a biological tragedy. Would someone please explain why it's so important in state standards and assessment programs for students to know the sequence of letters that spell a word but not the sequence of notes that constitute a melody? Why would our brain develop the capability to process both major communicative languages if they're not biologically important? *Motherese* song thrives before speech begins.

Music and dance are deeply and aesthetically integrated, and especially with adolescents. A spoken message is enhanced by the body language of gesture and facial expression, and a musical message is enhanced by the body language of dance. We want to *dance* with those to whom we send our positive musical expressions. Dance uses choreographed and improvisational movements. Previous generations were more apt to focus on choreographed dance movements, but contemporary adolescent dance (like music) is more improvisational, free-form.

We can think of both ballet and sports such as basketball and hockey as collaborative dance forms—stories told by a group through choreographed and improvisational movements. Both formats typically tell a story of overcoming obstacles in order to achieve a desired end.

Competitive and aesthetic movement is so important to human life that the whole world gathers every two years to see who can move the best. Some Olympic events involve speed and distance competitions, but others (such as gymnastics and figure skating) focus more on the aesthetics of the movements. One could cynically suggest that much of the Winter Olympics is basically about standing on a board or sitting in a tub and letting gravity take over—but that would miss the whole joie de vivre of skiing and sledding.

Aesthetics emerge quickly in our childhood exploration of movement. For example, a child is initially content to simply move on a skateboard, but the seemingly innate need to also do it with style and grace emerges quickly after basic mastery. Skateboarding soon becomes dancing on wheels. Similarly, piano scales meld into marvelous melodies; basic drawing skills draw out perceptual aesthetics; mud pies become ceramics. We humans don't just move to move—and we handsomely reward those whose virtuoso movements make our spirits soar.

Folks don't pay steep admission prices to watch pro basketball players merely pass the ball and throw it through the hoop more often than their opponents. *How* the players pass and shoot baskets is what draws spectators—and pro players have been honing their basketball aesthetics for most of their lives.

Music and sports are central to adolescence. Adolescents enjoy doing both, and when they're older, they'll nostalgically watch another generation of adolescents play the games they enjoyed playing, and they'll flock to nostalgic concerts of the musicians who helped to define their adolescence. When my wife and I go dancing, we can always tell who will get up to dance when the band plays a song—those who were adolescents when the song was composed.

THE HUMANITIES

Although the arts in their various forms may include a verbal component, they tend to emphasize nonverbal forms of communication. The humanities and drama focus principally on verbal (and frequently narrative) explorations of the human condition. We're storytellers, and we also like to hear the stories of the experiences others have had. A childhood without such stories is a bleak childhood indeed.

Adolescence provides an opportunity to leave home and relate our life story to nonkin friends and potential mates. Throughout our life span, we learn as much about ourselves through such personal narratives as others learn about us. Adolescents also spend a lot of time attending to the dramatic narratives of fictional people. The books, plays, films, and TV programs that interest them the most tend to relate to their own adolescence. Judy Blume's novels on the concerns of adolescent girls are a good example of the power of narrative in explaining the factual underpinnings of such issues as body image and sexuality.

Like the arts, the humanities provide opportunities to experience challenges metaphorically when we're not confronted with them in their real form, and so they also help us to develop and maintain the emotion, attention, and problem-solving systems and strategies we'll use when we actually confront the challenge. As implied earlier, the arts and humanities thus often play an important arousal/focusing role in society that's analogous to the role that emotion/attention play in individuals. Picasso's mural *Guernica* and Aristophanes's drama *Lysistrata* are renowned examples from the arts and humanities that alerted (and continue to alert) society to culturally important dangers and opportunities—in both examples, to the horrors of war. What dramatic forms will emerge out of the current Middle East conflicts? The probability is high that current adolescents will develop them—if we teach them how to understand, appreciate, and develop drama.

Chapter 5 discussed cognitive differences in processing factual information and making adaptive choices. The arts and humanities involve unique expressions that are centered on preference. It's possible to precisely and objectively evaluate factual information ($6 \times 5 = 30$) but not artistic expression. If it were possible to precisely and objectively evaluate art, it's not art but rather reproducible craft. There's nothing wrong with craft; it's just not art. When a noted pianist was asked to explain the difference between a piano player and a pianist, he responded that anyone could play the correct notes. That response gets to the heart of the issue. Playing the correct notes is important, but the aesthetics of playing the correct notes with preferential (adaptive) style and grace are more important.

Consider the professional basketball illustration above. Factual information (such as scores, averages, and records) dominates sports reporting. Fans want their team to win, but they're generally more interested in observing the many choices that occur during a game—as elite players follow set plays or improvise shots, coaches send players in and out of the game, and referees respond to or ignore violations. Perhaps more important, fans want both teams to play with the creative style and grace expected of athletic virtuosos. It will thus be possible to identify the champion with factual certainty at the end of the NBA playoffs, but something is seriously missing in the enterprise if that's all the long season was about.

Similarly, there's something seriously missing in an adolescent's development if the creative essence is missing that emerges through exploratory experiences with the arts and humanities. An adolescent is reaching for autonomy, and reaching isn't a completed action. It's rather an action in process. It's something important to ponder in an era that's increasingly concerned with rigid educational standards and precise assessments.

CHAPTER NINE

Collaboration and Autonomy

Going Beyond Adolescence

The recurring necessary expressions *goodbye* and *hello* may well be the two most important statements made by individuals within a social species. The periodic loss of family and friends and the consequent need to establish and maintain new relationships are among the most stressful challenges we humans confront. We also say goodbye and hello to belief systems (such as religious and political affiliations), to geographic areas, to jobs, and to life stages. We thus say goodbye and hello very often over our life spans—especially during adolescence, when we fine-tune our personal and social identities, and stressful distractions and decisions abound.

Chapters 2, 6, and 7 discussed elements of stress. To complete the discussion, the stress response emerged as a short-term, high-energy physical response to an imminent, survival-level danger or opportunity. Danger leads to fearful distress, and opportunity leads to optimistic eustress. Both forms of stress are related, in that they both require a similar major expenditure of adaptive energy. For example, activities such as skiing that expend a lot of energy are stressfully dangerous because we can get injured, but they're also a stressfully exhilarating opportunity to get out and activate our entire body. Similarly, the confrontation between a predator and its prey will activate stress responses in both—eustress for the eventual winner and distress for the eventual loser.

We often inappropriately activate a stress response for challenges that don't require a heightened physical response. For example, both losing a job (goodbye) and getting a job (hello) can activate a stress response that inappropriately diverts the cognitive energy needed for an effective vocational response to the fear-driven tension that accomplishes nothing relative to the new vocational reality. Such stress wouldn't be worrisome in the short run, but Chapter 7 reported that the chronic activation of a stress response to resolve social and cultural dilemmas negatively affects the robustness of brain systems that regulate rational thought and behavior.

Many of the stressors that currently beset us (and especially adolescents) are social or cultural. Death or divorce within our family, job problems, spiteful remarks, the breakup of a friendship, and commuter driving can all cause distress. On the positive (eustress) side of the equation, moving to a new school or neighborhood could activate a stress response, even if it's an improvement over our current situation. A stress response can fuel the excitement we feel when we've won a major challenge or award. The birth of a baby is generally stressful, but the circumstances will determine if it's distress or eustress. But in all these situations, nothing is gained biologically by increasing large-muscle tension, decreasing digestive processes, and tamping down our immune systems.

The typical adolescent lack of mature judgment can thus result in the impulsive expenditure of biologically expensive stress energy for a personal or social challenge, such as a friend's presumed snub. Such situations are better resolved through rational thought and/or negotiation. Unfortunately, the frontal lobes that process rational problem-solving decisions are developing but are not yet mature during adolescence. When folks talk about raging adolescent hormones, they're generally referring to an inappropriate stress response to a problem that most adults would consider minor.

The central challenge of adolescence is the two-part integration of the issues the previous chapters explored. This integration focuses on the development of personal and social identities that allow an adolescent to collaborate pleasantly and effectively with others while still maintaining the integrity of a developing personal autonomy. These are the two sides of the adolescent coin.

COLLABORATION

We don't get to select our birth family, and our initial very dependent childhood provides no easy escape from it. It's thus important for children to develop a compatible relationship with the family, and unfortunately, some young children have to determine how best to survive in an abusive family situation.

Birth also inserts us into the broader culture that encompasses our family, such as the community's location and socioeconomic status and its dominant belief systems. Again, children tend to simply accept and accommodate to the existing cultural mores, since most have experienced only their current culture.

We may be born into a democratic society, but we have to learn how to collaborate as citizens. Family and school must thus both develop democratic skills in young people, and adolescence should build on a substantial childhood foundation.

Authoritarian governments have dominated much of human history. The representative form of democracy initiated in the United States was a bold political experiment that has taken more than 200 years to develop, and it is still continuously evolving through challenges by individuals, groups, and events. Our democratic society, like a family, is characterized as much by disagreement as by agreement—but we've learned over the years how to disagree without being unduly disagreeable. A majority vote in a democracy settles the disagreement, but the minority can seek redress through the courts and subsequent elections. Individual thought and expression are constitutionally protected, and governments change by vote rather than by force.

The rest of the world observed as we gradually worked out the kinks in the system, and an increasing number liked what they saw. About a dozen other democracies had emerged by the beginning of the 20th century, and today 120 of the some 200 countries in the world have some form of democratic government. One can expect that the movement toward democratic forms of government will increase as ease of travel and electronic communication combine to turn the world into an even more democratically collaborative global village than it currently is.

John Dewey's eloquent argument at the beginning of the 20th century that maturing citizens in a democratic society deserve a democratically run school seemed reasonable to many, but the movement had all but died by midcentury. Curriculum and management were viewed by most as administrative functions—the adults managed the students. Our democratic society needed intelligent autonomous citizens, but it also needed a compliant workforce who would show up on time and do what supervisors asked them to do. The school seemed a good place to teach that. We thus maintained an authoritarian school system within a democratic society, despite the apparent contradiction. The family similarly tended toward an authoritarian model.

The serious shift toward a democratic school occurred gradually during the second half of the 20th century via a variety of school experiments. Educators began to realize that classroom management could be viewed as a curricular rather than an administrative function—a social laboratory in which students could collaborate on many of the mundane-to-important decisions that teachers typically make and develop important problem-solving, negotiation, and citizenship skills in the process. School is the only institution in our society in which young folks interact for 13 years with many hundreds of nonkin at a similar developmental stage. What are the options if our society doesn't explicitly develop social and democratic skills within its schools? Parenting models have similarly emerged in recent years that encourage greater child participation in family decisions.

The shift from a 20th-century society focused on making and moving objects to a 21st-century society focused more on creating and moving *information* suggests that collaborative behavior may become as valued within the 21st-century workforce as compliant behavior. As Chapter 4 suggested, a democratic school and family encourage an independent, entrepreneurial spirit—and help to develop the requisite skills.

A democratic management model doesn't absolve parents and educators from responsibility. We're a representative democracy, and parents and educators represent society in its desire to maintain a safe, effective living and learning environment. Individuals in a democracy aren't free to do anything they want. Freedom isn't license. Still, the entire family and class group can democratically make many decisions that parents and educators now make—if we would put our minds to it. Parents and teachers soon discover that when they make all the management decisions, they are worn out by the end of the day, and their children and students are bored and/or surly.

A democratic management model won't solve all the behavior problems that young people and adults commit. Misbehavior occurs within all management models—and our representative democracy functions effectively with all sorts of misbehavior. For example, democracies have an adult version of *"time-out"* called prison. Our body/brain and our government are both behaviorally excellent but not perfect.

Democratic procedures work, despite a constant messy pattern of disagreement and inefficiency, because a democracy is tuned to the striking similarities that biological and social systems exhibit. Managing a country, family, or classroom is functionally similar to body/brain management. We're biased toward challenge, in that most of our emotions are negative, and much of our cognitive energy is focused on solving problems. When things are running smoothly, we tend to go looking for trouble—at the personal, community, and national levels.

In more than 200 years we've not discovered a magic formula for creating a democracy at the national, family, or classroom level. Developing a perfect formula misses the whole point of the enterprise. A democracy is an unfinished process replete with dangers and opportunities, and our social nature prefers a continuing collaborative search for the solutions.

Our nation began with a determination to succeed as a democracy and then worked collaboratively to temporarily solve each successive challenge it confronted. Every constitutional amendment and legislative act represents something that wasn't previously right.

Parents and educators should similarly begin their shift to a truly democratic family or classroom with honest collaborations that solve simple issues that arise and go on from there. Think of all the family and classroom decisions related to space, time, and movement. Think of all the decisions related to who gets to make the decision and how much energy and resources should be expended on the project. Think of all the decisions related to what's possible and what's appropriate. Young people who are encouraged to collaborate in these simple family and classroom decisions will mature into adults who can collaborate on analogous civic decisions.

School, community, and religious organizations provide many opportunities for adolescents to learn and practice the leadership and membership skills that enhance social interaction. Classroom cooperative learning projects and school celebratory events (such as proms and homecoming) provide similar opportunities for adolescents to get involved at whatever level they wish. Further, adolescents spend a lot of time and energy planning and running the informal social events that dominate their lives. The point is that a broad formal and informal cultural framework already exists for the development of collaborative skills. The challenge for adult mentors is to encourage adolescent participation.

THE REACH FOR AUTONOMY

We're a social species, but we're also individuals, and so our push for individual identity and expression is strong, and it emerges early. No two children in a family or classroom are identical, even though they're all members of the same family or class. Uniqueness within similarities is a central property of biology. No two leaves on a maple tree are identical, but it's easy to identify all of them as maple leaves.

Children spend a lot of time observing others, from peers to adults. Their mirror neuron system provides them with an automatic mental model of the thought processes and intentions of others, and so it simplifies the cultural mimicking that's necessary in maturation. We're not doomed to a mimicking existence, however, since the human *dance* is defined as much by improvisation as by choreography. Chapter 6 suggested that play and games are principal childhood and adolescent explorations of creative individual expression within cultural parameters and peer comparison.

A sense of self emerges through such constant observation and activity. Self-concept refers to the way in which we define ourselves, and self-esteem refers to the value we place on that definition. Most young people can easily determine who is an almost equal competitor and who is someone to observe and emulate. Therefore, they don't necessarily consider themselves failures if others surpass them. Further, they may be interested in observing others excel in a certain activity (such as basketball) but have no real desire to participate in it themselves.

The adolescent *goodbyes* to childhood and family are balanced by their *hellos* to adolescence and peer friendships. Their reach for autonomy often begins informally with childhood expressions of interest and aptitude. Hobbies, musical talent, and sports skills are examples of specialties through which young people begin to distance themselves from peers. It's important for us to be good at something and to eventually become so good that we control the specialty rather than being controlled by it.

It's not uncommon for adolescents to become cynical—to believe that the world is full of phonies. Childhood dependence on parents, teachers, and other adults is a necessary reality because children lack the personal judgment to question many of the decisions adults make. Frontal lobe maturation brings the realization that most problems have multiple solutions, and so it's not surprising that this periodically results in disenchantment with family, political, and educational decisions that adolescents had earlier considered to be legitimate. It's another step toward adult autonomy.

Most young people will have often said goodbye and hello by the time they're full-blown adolescents. A divorce or the death of a parent, a family job-related move, and the move from a neighborhood elementary school to a regional secondary school are all examples of life changes that young people experience but don't control. Most adults can recall the point during their adolescence when they simply wanted to take control over as much of their life as they could—but to do it with good friends. That's the essence of the reach for autonomy.

You play an important modeling role in this journey. Adolescents tend to carefully observe the adults in their lives and incorporate what they can from their positive and negative observations. If you want an adolescent to be truthful, be truthful. If you want an adolescent to be friendly, be friendly. If you want an adolescent to be productive, be productive. It doesn't necessarily follow that the adolescent will embrace values and behaviors that you consider positive, but you'll know that you did your best.

This book began with the observation that no simple recipe exists for parents, educators, and other adults on how best to mentor a young person through adolescence, beyond thinking of it as a true mentoring experience—a few general principles integrated into a lot of unconditional love and collaborative improvisation. Genuine collaborative trust during childhood lays the foundation for a continuing genuine collaborative trust during adolescence. Human society wouldn't really be enhanced by a smooth, compliant adolescence. Each adolescent is a unique mix of joy and grief, pride and fear, accomplishment and failure. They drive the adults in their lives to delightful distraction, but then we also drove adults to delightful distraction during our adolescence.

This book ends similarly with no simple directions for how best to graduate from adolescence into autonomous adulthood. Some folks reach adult autonomy relatively early and successfully, and alas, some never seem to achieve it.

What this book focused on are explanations, models, metaphors, and commentaries that you might effectively use and adapt in your interactions with the adolescents in your life. These talking points emerge out of the long history that adolescents and adults have had with each other and out of the intriguing insights that are now emerging out of the cognitive neurosciences. It's a beginning.

The artist Paul Klee once suggested that a line is a dot that went for a walk. Leave it to an artist to characterize so concisely something that's as biologically and culturally complex as an adolescent journey.

We each get to make the adolescent journey once, and then we get to observe others make their journey. What more could one want from life?

Appendix A

Neurotransmitters and Neural Transmission

All functional elements in our body (from arteries to bones to cells and on up the alphabet) are constructed of molecules, principally protein molecules. Molecules are constructed from two or more bonded atoms—and in our brain, these atoms are principally carbon, oxygen, nitrogen, and hydrogen. The 50 or so neurotransmitters that scientists have already identified are a class of molecules that are mobile (such as blood) rather than stationary (such as bone). Blood carries nutrients throughout our body, and neurotransmitters carry *information* not only throughout our brain but also from and into our body's sensorimotor and glandular systems. A neurotransmitter's information is coded into its shape, chemistry, and distribution patterns.

Neurotransmitters stimulate, inhibit, or modulate the actions of other neurons, glands, and muscles. A neurotransmitter carries either an excitatory message that increases the subsequent activity of the receiving cell or an inhibitory message that helps to reduce it. The chemical composition of the neurotransmitter interacting with its target receptor determines the nature and complexity of the message.

All this molecular activity takes place in the synapse, a narrow gap between the terminal of the axon extension of the presynaptic neuron (the sending neuron) and receptors on a dendrite or the cell body of the postsynaptic neuron (the receiving neuron). A receptor is a protein molecule that projects through a dendrite's membrane and thus moves the chemical information of an attached neurotransmitter into the cell body.

Why do our brain's neurons need dozens of different types of neurotransmitters to communicate two basic verblike messages? *Send a message* or *Don't send a message.* Perhaps for the same reason that our language has dozens of verbs to express the basic message *Move your body by moving your legs,* when the verb *walk* expresses the basic idea. Words such as *run, dance, hop, jog,* and *skip* add information to the basic concept. Think also of the modulating effects of adverbs on verbs (such as *run quickly* or *dance exuberantly*). Similarly, the variety and complexity of excitatory and inhibitory neurotransmitters probably add some form of currently ill-understood supplementary information to the basic molecular message.

Our brain's neural activity is much more inhibitory than excitatory. At any given moment, we focus our attention, limit our activity, and ignore most of our memories. Imagine life with a principally excitatory brain that continually attends to everything, carries out all possible actions, and has continual access to all prior experiences! Inhibitory controls aren't well developed during childhood and early adolescence, and this causes many behavioral problems related to impulsivity and uncoordinated movements.

Almost all our brain's 50+ types of neurotransmitters can be classified chemically into the three following categories.

AMINO ACIDS

Amino acids are composed of 10 to 30 atoms, and 20 different kinds of amino acids constitute the building blocks of all proteins and neurotransmitters. Four chemically simple amino acids form one class of neurotransmitters. Glutamate and aspartate are excitatory neurotransmitters. Gamma-amniobutyric acid (GABA) and glycine are inhibitory neurotransmitters. Glutamate (send) and GABA (don't send) are the principal verblike neurotransmitters in the cerebral cortex. Glycine is a major neurotransmitter in the brain stem and spinal cord.

MONOAMINES

The six types of monoamine neurotransmitters are acetylcholine, dopamine, histamine, norepinephrine (or noradrenaline), epinephrine, and serotonin. They are chemically modified amino acids that act more slowly than the amino acid neurotransmitters. Each type is synthesized in a single subcortical source, and its circuitry spreads widely from there throughout our brain (think of a small lawn sprinkler that distributes water to a large area of lawn). The monoamines modulate the actions of the amino acid neurotransmitters (just as adverbs modulate verbs). The interaction of a monoamine neurotransmitter with its postsynaptic receptor helps to determine the nature of the message.

Chapter 7 discusses how psychoactive drugs alter the actions of various kinds of neurotransmitters. For example, alcohol affects the GABA system, nicotine affects the acetylcholine system, cocaine affects the dopamine system, methamphetamine affects the norepinephrine system, and hallucinatory drugs such as LSD affect the serotonin system.

PEPTIDES

The largest and most complex neurotransmitters are the peptides (or neuropeptides), such as oxytocin, vasopressin, and endorphin. They are composed of chains of 2 to 39 amino acids. Most of the dozens of types of neurotransmitters in our brain and peripheral nervous system are peptides, but their concentrations are much lower than those of the amino acids and monoamines (which are also known as the *classical neurotransmitters*). Many neurons that distribute a specific classical neurotransmitter also distribute a peptide that increases or decreases the postsynaptic neuron's receptivity of the neuron's primary transmitter—thus modulating its effect.

Peptides use neural networks, our circulatory system, and air passages to travel throughout our body and brain to modulate our broad range of pleasure and pain. A peptide action that occurs simultaneously in a large number of related cells can powerfully affect the decisions we make within the continuum of emotionally charged approaching and retreating behaviors, such as to drink/urinate, agree/disagree, buy/sell, and marry/divorce. In effect, the shifts in the body and brain levels of these molecules help to determine such cognitive decisions as what to do, when to do it, and how much energy to expend on the activity.

A peptide's message can vary in different body/brain areas, just as a two-by-four can be used in many different ways in the construction of a house. For example, angiotensin is a peptide that activates the seeking and conserving behaviors that regulate our body's fluid levels. In our brain, it does this principally by activating feelings of thirst and the consequent behaviors that seek water. In our body, it causes kidneys to conserve water. The situation is similar with many drugs. For example, alcohol can excite or sedate, depending on the amount ingested and the drinker's emotional state. Endorphin (and morphine, its drug equivalent) can similarly reduce intense pain and increase euphoria.

Although the neural transmission process is a bit more complicated than the following analogy, think of a postsynaptic receptor as a lock and a neurotransmitter as a key. The shape of the neurotransmitter (key) interacts with the shape of the receptor (lock). If it's a good match, the neurotransmitter transmits its excitatory or inhibitory message into the postsynaptic neuron. And like a key that's returned to one's pocket after opening the door, many neurotransmitters are pumped back into the presynaptic terminal after release from the receptor and used again.

Synapses are continuously busy, with a multitude of neurotransmitters arriving from various neurons within a neural network. If the number and intensity of the various molecular messages that simultaneously enter a postsynaptic neuron reach the postsynaptic neuron's firing threshold (think of a thermostat), the chemical message translates into an impulse that travels rapidly along the axon (think of an electrical charge traveling along a wire). When the impulse reaches the presynaptic axon terminal, it releases stored neurotransmitters into the synapse, where they cross to the postsynaptic dendrite receptors, and the communication process thus continues from neuron to neuron within a processing network.

One type of glial cell (an oligodendrocyte) wraps itself around long axons, creating an insulating layer called **myelin**. This speeds up the transmission of messages among related neurons, thus creating more efficient processing systems. Myelination is an important part of the adolescent maturation of efficient neuronal networks. Multiple sclerosis results from a breakdown of myelin and is characterized by a loss of processing efficiency.

Appendix B

The Cerebral Cortex

Our brain's deeply folded, six-layer cerebral cortex is organized both horizontally and vertically (see Figure B.1). To simplify a complex organizational process, information coming into a cortical region enters into Layer 4; internal processing of the information occurs in Layers 1 to 3; and the outgoing response leaves from Layers 5 and 6.

Much of the cortex is also organized vertically into hundreds of millions of highly interconnected, hair-thin (100-neuron) minicolumns that extend vertically through the six cortical layers (called the *gray matter*). Each minicolumn is specialized to process a very specific unit of information (such as to recognize a horizontal line or a specific tone). One hundred adjacent minicolumns combine into a unit to form a macrocolumn (about the thickness of the lead in a pencil) that can process more complex functions related to the minicolumns it incorporates (perhaps to help differentiate between the thickness of lines). Thousands of related macrocolumns form into one of the 50+ anatomically and functionally distinct areas that each brain hemisphere contains. Think of a library with many related books (such as the history or science books) shelved in a specific library section.

The axons in columnar neurons extend down the column through the cortical layers into the *white matter,* a dense web

Figure B.1   Schematic of Cortical Section

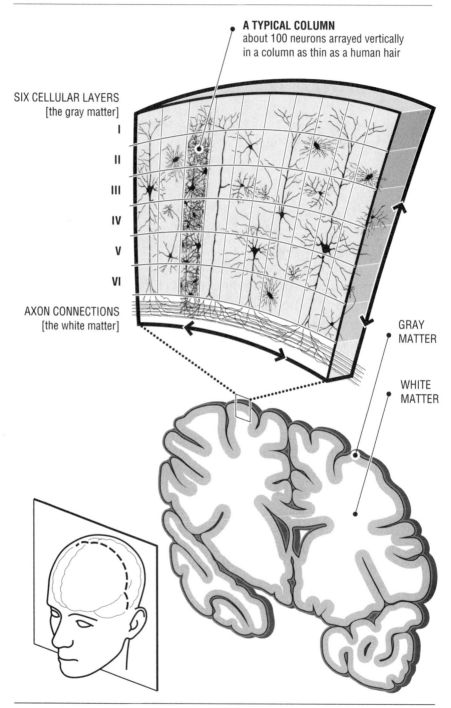

A TYPICAL COLUMN
about 100 neurons arrayed vertically
in a column as thin as a human hair

SIX CELLULAR LAYERS
[the gray matter]

I
II
III
IV
V
VI

AXON CONNECTIONS
[the white matter]

GRAY MATTER

WHITE MATTER

of axon extensions beneath the gray matter. The axons eventually leave the white matter to connect with neurons in a related nearby column or to extend into a column or system elsewhere in our brain or body.

Discrete columnar brain areas and systems thus process basic limited cognitive functions. These are incorporated into larger, specialized, widely distributed but highly interconnected areas and systems that collaborate on complex cognitive tasks. To extend the discussion in Chapter 2, our visual system has about 30 separate columnar subsystems that process such visual properties as shape, depth, color, quantity, and movement. The subsystem that responds to the color red processes it on every red object we see, and the subsystem that responds to circular shapes processes balls, compact disks, tires, doughnuts, and so on. Several of these subsystems will combine to process our perception of a rolling red ball or a flying blue Frisbee.

The interconnected columnar system in the cortex is analogous to the organization of a book. The approximately 100 cells in a column (gray matter) would represent the content on the pages of a book, and the axon extensions to other columns (white matter) would represent the bibliography that connects the book to other related published books and journals.

The more encompassing term *cerebrum* is commonly used to identify the combined gray and white matter of both hemispheres.

Glossary

Adrenal glands   Paired endocrine glands located above each kidney that produce adrenaline and cortisol, which fuel a stress response.

Amygdala   A pair of almond-shaped structures located in the lower front area of the two temporal lobes. They respond to sensory information that portends danger.

Anterior cingulate   *See* Cingulate.

Axon   A neuron's tubular extension that transmits information from the neuron cell body to other neurons in a network.

Brain stem   The finger-size structure at the base of the brain that regulates such survival functions as circulation, respiration, and endocrine gland activity, and relays sensorimotor information between body and brain.

Caudate nucleus   An important element of the brain's processing circuitry for movement, pleasure, and reward (located deep within the brain). It's thus active during expressions of romantic love.

Cerebellum   A two-hemisphere structure located behind the brain stem, tucked under the cerebral hemispheres. It plays a number of important roles in planning and executing behaviors, including the smooth regulation of automatic movements (such as walking).

Cerebral cortex   The large, deeply folded top layer of our brain that processes conscious thought and action. See Appendix B for an extended description.

Cingulate   A processing system located above the corpus callosum that integrates information from many brain areas in the resolution of ambiguous challenges.

Corpus callosum   A communicative band of more than 200 million myelinated axons that connects the two cerebral hemispheres.

Cortex   *See* Cerebral cortex.

Cortical   Refers to the cerebral cortex.

Cortisol   A hormone secreted by the adrenal glands that elevates our response capabilities during stressful challenges.

Dendrites   The large number of short tubular extensions from a neuronal cell body that receive molecular (neurotransmitter) information from the axons of other neurons.

DNA (deoxyribonucleic acid)   A ladder-shaped, meter-long, twisted and folded, self-replicating molecule that forms much of the nucleus of every cell. All cells (except egg, sperm, and red blood cells) have identical DNA molecules. DNA provides the genetic instructions for constructing and maintaining an organism, and it also transmits genetic information to an organism's subsequent generations.

Dopamine   An important monoamine neurotransmitter that helps to regulate emotional behaviors and conscious movements.

Endorphins   A class of peptide neurotransmitters (chemically related to opium and morphine) that reduce pain and enhance euphoria.

Estrogen   A steroid hormone that plays an important regulatory role in the female reproductive cycle and behavior. Estrogen is present in both females and males, but female levels are higher.

Frontal lobes   The front section of each of the two cerebral hemispheres. The frontal lobes play the central role in solving problems, making decisions, and initiating actions. They mature during the adolescent years.

Gene   A segment of DNA that contains the coded directions for assembling a protein molecule out of a unique combination of the 20 different kinds of amino acids.

Genome   The complete set of DNA genes in an organism. The approximately 30,000 human genes are incorporated into 23 separate pairs of chromosomes.

Glial cells   A system of perhaps a trillion cells that provide a variety of support services for neurons. The glial cells provide about half the mass of our brain, but they are much smaller than neurons.

Hemispheres   The two major right and left sections of the cerebrum (an encompassing term for the large upper part of our brain). The cerebral cortex on the outside of our brain is composed principally of cells arranged in columns and layers (gray matter). Underneath is the vast network of axons that interconnect the columns (the white matter). See Appendix B for a more complete description.

Hormones   A variety of molecular messengers that are synthesized in endocrine glands and then travel via the bloodstream to body and brain systems that must respond to a specific internal or external challenge.

Hypothalamus   A structure in the center of our brain that directly and indirectly regulates most body functions. It's often called the *brain's brain*.

Mirror neurons   A class of neurons that primes voluntary movements but that also activates when we observe someone else carry out the same behavior.

Motor cortex   A 2-inch-wide band of neurons that initiates conscious movements. It stretches across our brain from ear to ear, with specific areas devoted to the various parts of our motor system.

Myelin   Glial cells that wrap around long neuronal axons to create the insulating layer that increases the efficiency of neuronal transmission. See Appendix A for a more complete description.

Neuron   A specialized cell that transmits information within our brain and between our brain and body. Neurons have many short dendrite extensions that receive information from other neurons and sensorimotor systems and a (typically single) longer axon extension that sends information to other neurons and sensorimotor systems.

Neurotransmitter   One of 50+ different kinds of molecules that transmit chemical information within our nervous system. See Appendix A for a more complete description.

Norepinephrine   The principal neurotransmitter for regulating blood pressure and activating stress-related responses. It's also called noradrenaline.

Nucleus accumbens   A structure within the dopamine circuitry that is associated with pleasure and reward and is strongly implicated in addiction.

Occipital lobes   Paired sensory lobes in the upper rear section of our cerebral cortex that process vision and related phenomena.

Orbitofrontal cortex   A frontal lobe processing system above our eyes that participates in the recognition of errors and determines the genuineness of observed behavior.

Oxytocin   A pituitary hormone that initiates the uterine contractions in childbirth and lactation in breast-feeding. It also enhances social and bonding behaviors. Oxytocin is present in both males and females, but female levels are higher.

Parietal lobes   Paired sensory lobes in the upper back section of our cerebral cortex that process touch sensations, body and joint orientation, and space/location relationships.

Pheromones   Hormonelike molecules that travel via the air or physical contact to transmit strong social and sexual messages within a species.

Pineal gland   A neuroendocrine gland that produces the melatonin that helps to regulate sleeping and waking states.

Pituitary gland   The pea-size, principal gland of the endocrine gland system. Located below the hypothalamus in our brain, it produces many specialized hormones that affect most glandular and body functions.

Prefrontal cortex   The frontal lobe area directly behind our forehead that plays the principal role in conscious planning and decision making. It's our brain's equivalent of a corporation's chief executive officer.

Septum   One of several brain systems that process feelings of pleasure.

Serotonin   A monoamine neurotransmitter that inhibits awkward and impulsive movements and so enhances smooth, fluid movements. Since movement is a central human property, elevated serotonin levels are associated with high self-esteem (and vice versa).

Somatosensory cortex   A narrow neuronal band just behind the motor cortex that processes the touch sensations received on individual body parts.

Subcortical systems   All brain matter that is located beneath the cerebral cortex.

Substantia nigra   The brain stem area that produces dopamine, which is then transported to the frontal lobes and other brain areas.

Synapse   The narrow gap between the axon terminal of a presynaptic neuron and the dendrite or cell body receptor of a postsynaptic neuron. Neurotransmitters released from the axon terminal diffuse across the gap and attach to dendrite or cellular receptors.

Temporal lobes   Paired sensory lobes on the back and side of the cerebral cortex that process hearing, smell, taste, language and music perception and comprehension, complex visual processing (such as face recognition), and memory.

Testosterone   A steroid hormone associated principally with male reproductive behavior and with the escalation of behavior that is already aggressive. Testosterone is present in both males and females, but male levels are higher.

Vasopressin   A pituitary hormone that helps to regulate water retention and blood pressure. It also enhances social and bonding behaviors. Vasopressin is present in both males and females, but male levels are higher.

References and Resources

RECENT PRINT RESOURCES
FOR GENERAL READERS

Ackerman, D. (2004). *An alchemy of mind: The marvel and mystery of the brain.* New York: Charles Scribner's Sons.

Alexandrowicz, H. (2001). *Testing your mettle: Tough problems and real-world solutions for middle and high school teachers.* Thousand Oaks, CA: Corwin Press.

Andreasen, N. (2001). *Brave new brain: Conquering mental illness in the era of the genome.* New York: Oxford University Press.

Andreasen, N. (2005). *The creating brain: The neuroscience of genius.* New York: Dana Press.

Balog, D. (2003). *The Dana sourcebook of brain science: Resources for secondary and post-secondary teachers and students* (3rd ed.). New York: Dana Press.

Baron-Cohen, S. (2003). *The essential difference: The truth about the male and female brain.* New York: Basic Books.

Bloom, F., Beal, M., & Kupfer, D. (2002). *The Dana guide to brain health.* New York: Free Press.

Caine, R., Caine, G., McClintic, C., & Klimek, K. (2005). *12 brain/mind learning principles in action: The fieldbook for making connections, teaching, and the human brain.* Thousand Oaks, CA: Corwin Press.

Damasio, A. (2003). *Looking for Spinoza: Joy, sorrow, and the feeling brain.* New York: Harcourt.

Deasy, R. (Ed.). (2002). *Critical links: Learning in the arts and student academic and social development.* Washington, DC: Arts Education Partnership.

Dissanayake, E. (2000). *Art and intimacy: How the arts began.* Seattle: University of Washington Press.

Fisher, H. (2004). *Why we love: The nature and chemistry of romantic love.* New York: Henry Holt.

Gardner, H. (2004). *Changing minds: The art and science of changing our own and other people's minds.* Boston: Harvard Business School Press.

Gardner, H., Csikzentmihalyi, M., & Damon, W. (2001). *Good work: When excellence and ethics meet.* New York: Basic Books.

Gazzaniga, M. (2005). *The ethical brain.* New York: Dana Press.

Givens, B. (2002). *Teaching to the brain's natural learning systems.* Alexandria, VA: Association for Supervision and Curriculum Development.

Gladwell, M. (2005). *Blink: The power of thinking without thinking.* New York: Little, Brown.

Goldberg, E. (2005). *The wisdom paradox: How your mind can grow stronger while your brain grows older.* New York: Gotham Books.

Hawkins, J. (2004). *On intelligence: How a new understanding of the brain will lead to the creation of truly intelligent machines.* New York: Henry Holt.

Ivey, G., & Fisher, D. (2006). *Creating literacy-rich schools for adolescents.* Alexandria, VA: Association for Supervision and Curriculum Development.

Jensen, E. (2004). *Teaching with the brain in mind.* Alexandria, VA: Association for Supervision and Curriculum Development.

Johnson, S. (2005). *Everything bad is good for you: How today's popular culture is actually making us smarter.* New York: Riverhead Books.

Jones, S. (2003). *Blueprint for student success: A guide to research-based teaching practices K–12.* Thousand Oaks, CA: Corwin Press.

Kohn, A. (2005). *Unconditional parenting: Moving from rewards and punishments to love and reason.* New York: Atria Books.

Levitin, D. (2006). *This is your brain on music: The science of a human obsession.* New York: Dutton.

McEwen, B., & Lasley, E. (2002). *The end of stress as we know it.* New York: Dana Press.

Mithen, S. (2006). *The singing Neanderthals: The origins of music, language, mind, and body.* Cambridge, MA: Harvard University Press.

Provine, R. (2001). *Laughter: A scientific investigation.* New York: Viking Press.

Quartz, S., & Sejnowski, T. (2002). *Liars, lovers, and heroes: What the new brain science reveals about how we become who we are.* New York: William Morrow.

Ratey, J. (2001). *A user's guide to the brain.* New York: Pantheon Books.

Restak, R. (2002). *The secret life of the brain.* Washington, DC: Joseph Henry Press.

Restak, R. (2003). *The new brain: How the modern age is rewiring your mind.* New York: Rodale Press.

Sapolsky, R. (2004). *Why zebras don't get ulcers: An updated guide to stress, stress-related diseases, and coping* (3rd ed.). New York: Owl Books.

Schacter, D. (2001). *The seven sins of memory: How the mind forgets and remembers.* New York: Houghton Mifflin.

Sousa, D. (2001). *How the brain learns.* Thousand Oaks, CA: Corwin Press.

Sprenger, M. (2006). *Becoming a "wiz" at brain-based teaching* (2nd ed.). Thousand Oaks, CA: Corwin Press.

Sternberg, R. (1996). *Successful intelligence: How practical and creative intelligence determine success in life.* New York: Simon & Schuster.

Stone, R. (2002). *Best practices for high school classrooms: What award-winning secondary teachers do.* Thousand Oaks, CA: Corwin Press.

Strauch, B. (2003). *The primal teen: What the new discoveries about the teenage brain tell us about our kids.* New York: Doubleday.

Sylwester, R. (2003). *A biological brain in a cultural classroom: Enhancing cognitive and social development through collaborative classroom management.* Thousand Oaks, CA: Corwin Press.

Sylwester, R. (2005). *How to explain a brain: An educator's handbook of brain terms and cognitive processes.* Thousand Oaks, CA: Corwin Press.

Taylor, S. (2002). *The tending instinct: How nurturing is essential to who we are and how we live.* New York: Times Books.

Thornburg, D. (2002). *The new basics: Education and the future of work in the telematic age.* Alexandria, VA: Association for Supervision and Curriculum Development.

Wolfe, P. (2001). *Brain matters: Translating research into classroom practice.* Alexandria, VA: Association for Supervision and Curriculum Development.

Mass Circulation Magazines That Often Contain Articles on Adolescence and Cognitive Neuroscience Developments

Discover Magazine
New Scientist
Newsweek
The New Yorker
Psychology Today

Science News
Scientific American
Time
U.S. News & World Report

Nonprint Resources

Association for Supervision and Curriculum Development. (2006). *Teaching the Adolescent Brain.* Video or DVD program. www .ascd.org.

Cerebrum: The Dana forum on brain science. www.dana.org/books/ press/cerebrum.

Ramachandran, V. S. (2006). "Mirror Neurons and the Brain in the Vat." http://www.edge.org/3rd_culture/ramachandran06/ ramachandran06_index.html.

Useful Web Sites That Focus on Adolescence and Cognitive Neuroscience Information and Issues

Brain and Mind: Electronic Magazine on Neuroscience
http://www.epub.org/cm/home_i.htm
Focused on neuroscience education issues, but also useful for educators interested in the neurosciences.

Brain Connection
http://www.brainconnection.com
Very useful, nontechnical information on cognitive neuroscience issues for parents and educators. Brain Connection contains extensive descriptive/analytical reviews of most of the following recommended Web sites (click on *Web sites*).

BrainInfo Database
http://braininfo.rprc.washington.edu/mainmenu.html
A comprehensive resource on brain regions, terms, and processes.

Brainland: The Neuroscience Information Center
http://www.brainland.com
Professional information for the neuroscience community, but also quite a bit that's useful for educators interested in the neurosciences.

The Child Development Institute
http://www.cdipage.com
Useful information for parents on problems that children and adolescents confront.

CogNet: MIT Cognitive and Brain Science Community Online
http://cognet.mit.edu
   A wide range of useful information in an interactive format, sponsored by the Massachusetts Institute of Technology.

The Charles A. Dana Foundation
http://www.dana.org
   A broad, informative Web site suitable for both scientists and the general public. *Brainy Kids Online* is an especially useful section for educators.

Eric Chudler's Neuroscience Resource Site
http://faculty.washington.edu/chudler/ehceduc.html
   A very informative Web site, with links to many other Web sites. *See also* Chudler's other Web site, Neuroscience for Kids (below).

Girls in Training
http://www.girlsintraining.org
   Focuses on such areas as nutrition, fitness, self-esteem, and positive body image.

Neuroscience for Kids
http://faculty.washington.edu/chudler/neurok.html
   A marvelous resource of information and exploratory projects for young people. *See also* Eric Chudler's Neuroscience Resource Site (above).

Neuroguide.com
http://www.neuroguide.com
   A comprehensive access to Internet sites on brain issues. See especially *Best Bets*.

Public Broadcasting Service Teacher Source
www.pbs.org/teachersourcefocused
   Excellent resource for educators on many topics, including the cognitive neurosciences.

Raising Kids
http://www.raisingkids.co.uk
   A British Web site on practical issues related to child/adolescent rearing.

The Search Institute
http://www.search-institute.org
An independent, nonprofit organization dedicated to helping young people develop.

The Society for Neuroscience
http://www.sfn.org
The Web site of the professional society, but *Brain Backgrounders* and *Brain Briefings* are especially useful resources for educators.

The Washington University School of Medicine Neuroscience Tutorial
http://thalamus.wustl.edu/course
An excellent Internet tutorial on the brain and brain anatomy.

Whole Brain Atlas
http://www.med.harvard.edu/AANLIB/home.html
It's just what the title says—anything you could possibly want to know about the brain.

The World Wide Web Virtual Library: Neuroscience (Biosciences)
http://neuro.med.cornell.edu/VL
Links to just about any Web site one could imagine.

Index